Classics of
INDIAN
COOKING

NEW YORK

Published in USA 1985
by Exeter Books
Distributed by Bookthrift
Exeter is a trademark of Simon & Schuster
New York, New York

ISBN 0 671 07404 0

Printed and bound by Grafiche Editoriali Padane S.p.A.,
Cremona, Italy

Printed in Italy
ISBN 0 671 07404 0

Contents

Introduction

Indian cooking is a story of geography and of religion. The main cooking divisions can be separated, roughly but fairly satisfactorily, into north and south (with some deviations along the coast line), and many eating and cooking habits can be traced directly to the dietary restrictions of the main religions of the sub-continent; Moslem and Hindu.

The differences between the north and south are many. In the north, various waves of conquerors have come and gone and left their influence, some of their culture—and much of their food (except for the British, who built roads). The Moghuls, particularly, have left their mark on Indian cuisine and the rich diversity of their cooking still finds echoes in many of the finer dishes of the north to this day, such as Huseini Kebabs. The Persians also contributed their share, particularly their

fondness for rice-based dishes (many of the famous pulaos of the north are Persian in influence if not in origin). The northern cuisine evolved basically in the courts of the many royal princelings so it is not a cuisine of necessity but rather one that is rich with spices, herbs and sauces.

In the south, the outside influences are less obvious although the Portuguese have left traces of their occupation. The food is hotter, less subtle than in the north and rice is very much a staple of the diet—much more so than in the north. The south abounds in fresh vegetables and fruit, and both are not only incorporated into the cuisine but form the basis of many of the most popular dishes.

The south is predominantly Hindu, and in consequence vegetarian, although adherence to the stricter aspects of the faith vary

according to caste (the higher the caste the more strictly the adherence—the Brahmin are not supposed to eat eggs or fish as well as meat) and practical necessity (there are communities of Hindus along the coast who eat fish, which is plentiful there, claiming that it is not forbidden 'meat' but rather 'fruit of the sea' and therefore not taboo). But most of the people are at least vegetarian in that they do not eat meat and a vast and superb vegetarian cuisine has therefore developed in this area. In the absence of meat, pulses form an important part of the diet and simple lentil dishes such as Sambar and Khichri have become classics.

There are Hindus in the north too, but there the dietary laws are interpreted more leniently, only beef from the sacred cow being forbidden. In Pakistan, of course, where the population is predominantly Moslem, only pork is refused and both beef and lamb are much enjoyed.

The sub-continent has other minorities which have also made their culinary contribution. The Parsees, for instance, who settled many centuries ago in west India to escape religious persecution, are renowned for their cooking, and several of their dishes are now part of the standard Indian repertoire— Dhansak, an unusual combination of chicken

and lentils and Ekuri, a sort of spicy scrambled eggs dish, are perhaps the best known.
The Syrian Christians have contributed Vath, a ceremonial duck dish, and the Goans, descended at least in spirit from the Portuguese conquerors of their island, are famous for their seafood and for their almost soup-like curries.

Outside India, Indian cooking is often dismissed in one word—curry. Indeed most dishes are reckoned to taste very much the same, with perhaps the only variation being in the main ingredient. Nothing could be further from the truth. The 'curry' so misinterpreted in the west is, in fact, merely a corruption of the Tamil word for sauce and, correctly used, describes only one type of Indian stew, and one of the simplest in the cooking repertoire at that.

That the variety and range of Indian cooking is huge can be seen by even a quick perusal of the recipes which follow in this book. But what is perhaps not quite so apparent is the quite bewildering, and very sophisticated, number of different techniques or styles of cooking. *Tandoori* is probably the best known outside India and is simple in the extreme, being primarily based on four traditional dishes cooked in a clay oven called a *tandoor*, which is a popular feature in parts of north India.

And although other types of food are now cooked in this way, especially fish, the four (Tandouri Murg or Chicken, Boti Kebabs or lamb on skewers, and two types of bread) remain the standards. Recipes are given later in the book for the two meat recipes, which are adapted to standard ovens. *Biryanis* and *pulaos* are both dishes based on rice—in the former the meat ingredient predominates and the overall dish is more complicated and richer than is the custom in *pulaos*, although both dishes are north Indian in origin. Many versions of both dishes use saffron to give a subtle flavour—and colour—to the finished dish.

Other important techniques include *korma*, the name given to a method of braising, usually in yogurt, although cream can be used (lamb is the meat traditionally used although pork can be substituted); *vindaloo*, where vinegar is traditionally added to the spices to create a hot and slightly sour flavour; and *chasnidarh*, which is the Indian version of sweet and sour.

But the real glory and challenge of Indian cooking lies in obtaining just the 'right' combination of the many spices which go to create the flavour called 'curry'. The combination is called *masala*, and each of the components of a *masala* should be carefully measured so that it will retain its own particular flavour in the dish, yet combine with the other spices so that none predominates. (Occasionally, it will happen that, deliberately, one spice *will* be chosen to 'stand out', but this is the exception rather than the rule.) It is an art which, of necessity, must be practised by individual cooks until they attain the final flavour most pleasing to their palate. In many of the recipes which follow, whole spices are recommended for *masalas* rather than ground ones, simply because they retain their flavour longer. Like the final taste of the *masala*, however, it is left to the particular cook to decide which is used—they are of course interchangeable. If you intend to grind your own whole spices, it is worth reserving a specific pestle and mortar for this purpose.

Menus, as they are constructed in the west, are unknown in India and, as in China, the dishes to be presented at a meal are placed on the table together. On average, a main meal will consist of a meat and/or fish offering, with three or four vegetable dishes, usually including lentils or rice, and one or more of the Indian breads. Sweetmeats are usually served after the meal, and bowls of hot water are passed around afterwards so that guests may wash their hands. Traditionally each diner is served separately from a *thali*, or round tray, upon which are placed individual bowls of the food being served. It is considered extremely rude either to eat from someone else's *thali*, or to offer anything from your own.

Although knives and forks can be used to eat Indian food, in many areas the custom is to eat with your hands, or rather right hand. (The left being considered unclean and therefore used neither to eat nor to serve food). Depending on which part of the country you find yourself (and presumably your state of hunger), you will either delicately lower your fingers into the food and scoop it up, or plunge in with more or less your whole hand. In the south, meals are often served from banana leaves rather than bowls. Alcohol is not served during the meal, although in the west lager is sometimes drunk as an accompaniment. Tea is often served after the meal.

Whether you choose to serve Indian food according to the customs of the sub-continent or whether you serve it within the context of a western menu, is up to you; it is most versatile. For Indian cooking is easily mastered—and the rewards for doing so are great: delicious and 'different' meals, often at little cost, with a variety of tastes guaranteed to tempt even the most jaded of palates.

Vegetarian Dishes

Channa Dhal (curried chick-peas)—one of the glories of a superb Indian vegetarian cuisine. Served with a selection of other vegetable or lentil dishes, and some chutney or salad, it makes a delicious meal.

CHANNA DHAL
(Curried Chick-Peas)

	Metric/U.K.	U.S.
Dried chick-peas, soaked in cold water overnight and drained	350g/12oz	2 cups
Salt	1 tsp	1 tsp

Ghee or clarified butter	40g/1½oz	3 Tbs
Cumin seeds	1 tsp	1 tsp
Medium onion, chopped	1	1
Fresh root ginger, peeled and chopped	2½cm/1in piece	1in piece
Turmeric	1 tsp	1 tsp
Ground cumin	½ tsp	½ tsp
Ground coriander	1 tsp	1 tsp
Garam masala	1 tsp	1 tsp
Hot chilli powder	¼ tsp	¼ tsp
Chopped coriander leaves	1 Tbs	1 Tbs

Put the chick-peas in a saucepan and cover with about 1½l/2½ pints (6 cups) of water and

the salt. Bring to the boil. Reduce the heat to low, half-cover the pan and simmer for 1 hour.

Melt the ghee or clarified butter in a saucepan. Add the cumin seeds and cook for 1 minute. Add the onion and ginger and fry until the onion is golden brown.

Combine the turmeric, ground cumin, coriander, garam masala, and chilli powder with 2 tablespoons of water to make a smooth paste. Add the paste to the onion mixture in the pan and fry for 3 minutes, stirring constantly. Add the chick-peas and cooking liquid and bring the mixture to the boil, stirring constantly. Reduce the heat to low, cover and simmer for 30 minutes, or until the chick-peas are tender but still firm. Adjust the seasoning if necessary.

Transfer the mixture to a warmed serving dish and sprinkle over the coriander leaves before serving.

6 Servings

BAINGAN BHARTA
(Curried Aubergine [Eggplant] Purée)

Bhartas are popular all over northern India where they are served as part of a main meal, or as a sort of side 'salad'.

	Metric/U.K.	U.S.
Aubergines (eggplants)	1kg/2lb	2lb
Canned peeled tomatoes	425g/14oz	14oz
Ground coriander	2 tsp	2 tsp
Ground cumin	1 tsp	1 tsp
Turmeric	1 tsp	1 tsp
Chopped coriander leaves	2 Tbs	2 Tbs
Ghee or vegetable oil	5 Tbs	5 Tbs
Onion, finely chopped	1	1
Garlic cloves, crushed	2	2
Fresh root ginger, peeled and finely chopped	4cm/1½in piece	1½in piece
Green chilli, chopped	1	1
Salt	1 tsp	1 tsp
Juice of ½ lemon		

Preheat the oven to moderate 180°C (Gas Mark 4, 350°F).

Cut the aubergines (eggplants) in half, lengthways, and make two or three slits in the flesh. Place the halves, flesh side up, in a baking dish. Cover with foil and put the dish into the oven. Bake for 1 hour, or until they are soft. Remove from the oven and set aside to cool.

When the aubergines (eggplants) are cool enough to handle, scoop the pulp from the skins and transfer to a bowl. Discard the skins. Mash the pulp to a smooth purée, then beat in the tomatoes, coriander, cumin, turmeric and 1 tablespoon of the coriander leaves. Set aside.

Heat the ghee or oil in a large frying-pan. Add the onion and fry until it is soft. Stir in the garlic, ginger and chilli and fry for 5 minutes, stirring frequently. Stir in the aubergine (eggplant) mixture and salt and cook, stirring frequently, until the liquid has evaporated and the mixture is thick and smooth.

Transfer the bharta to a warmed serving dish, sprinkle over the lemon juice and remaining coriander leaves, and serve at once.

6 Servings

WENGYACHEN BHARIT
(Curried Aubergines [Eggplants])

	Metric/U.K.	U.S.
Aubergines (eggplants)	1kg/2lb	2lb
Butter	40g/1½oz	3 Tbs
Medium onions, finely chopped	3	3
Garlic cloves, crushed	4	4
Fresh root ginger, peeled and finely chopped	5cm/2in piece	2in piece
Green chillis, seeded and finely chopped	2	2
Coriander leaves, chopped	½ bunch	½ bunch
Turmeric	1 tsp	1 tsp
Ground cumin	1 tsp	1 tsp
Salt	1 tsp	1 tsp
Yogurt	175ml/6floz	¾ cup
Sugar	2 tsp	2 tsp

Preheat the oven to moderate 180°C (Gas Mark 4, 350°F).

Make three slits in each aubergine (eggplant) and arrange them in a baking dish. Put the dish into the oven and bake the aubergines (eggplants) for 1 hour, or until they are soft. Remove from the oven and set aside to cool.

*Vendai Kai Kari is
a southern Indian
vegetable dish which has
okra as the main
ingredient.*

When they are cool enough to handle, scoop the pulp from the skins and transfer to a bowl. Mash to a smooth purée. Discard the skins.

Melt the butter in a large saucepan. Add the onions and fry until they are golden brown. Stir in the garlic, ginger and chillis and fry for 3 minutes, stirring constantly. Stir in the coriander, turmeric and cumin. Cook for 1 minute, stirring constantly. Stir in the aubergine (eggplant) purée and salt. Cook for 5 minutes, stirring frequently.

Stir in the yogurt and sugar, then remove from the heat. Transfer to a warmed serving dish.

Serve at once.

4 Servings

PAKORAS
(Vegetable Fritters)

Pakoras are usually served as a snack in India, and although cauliflower has been used here, the dish may be made from any raw vegetable, or shrimps can also be used.

	Metric/U.K.	U.S.
Chick-pea flour	175g/6oz	1½ cups
Salt	1 tsp	1 tsp
Ground coriander	1 tsp	1 tsp
Cayenne pepper	1 tsp	1 tsp
Water	175-250ml/ 6-8floz	¾-1 cup
Medium cauliflower, broken into flowerets	1	1
Sufficient vegetable oil for deep-frying		

Sift the flour, salt, coriander and cayenne into a bowl. Gradually pour in enough of the water to make a smooth pouring batter, stirring constantly with a wooden spoon. Set aside for 30 minutes.

Add the cauliflower flowerets to the batter and turn and toss to coat well.

Fill a deep-frying pan one-third full with oil and heat until it reaches 185°C (360°F) on a deep-fat thermometer, or until a small cube of stale bread dropped into the oil turns golden in 50 seconds.

Carefully lower the flowerets, a few at a time, into the oil and fry for 3 to 4 minutes, or until they are crisp and golden brown. Remove from the oil and drain on kitchen towels.

Transfer the cooked flowerets to a warmed serving dish and serve at once.

4 Servings

VENDAI KAI KARI
(Curried Okra)

This spicy dish comes from south India. If you prefer a less pungent curry, seed the chillis before adding them to the dish.

	Metric/U.K.	U.S.
Tamarind	50g/2oz	¼ cup
Boiling water	250ml/8floz	1 cup
Vegetable oil	60ml/2½floz	5 Tbs
Okra, cut into pieces	700g/1½lb	1½lb
Medium onions, sliced	2	2
Fresh root ginger, peeled	2½cm/1in	1in
and finely chopped	piece	piece
Garlic cloves, crushed	2	2
Green chillis, chopped	2	2
Turmeric	1 tsp	1 tsp
Ground coriander	1 Tbs	1 Tbs
Coconut milk	300ml/10floz	1¼ cups
Salt	1 tsp	1 tsp
Mustard seeds	1 tsp	1 tsp
Curry or bay leaves	4	4

Put the tamarind into a small bowl and pour over the boiling water. Set aside until the mixture is cool. Pour the mixture through a strainer into a bowl, using the back of a wooden spoon to push through as much of the softened tamarind pulp as possible. Pour over a little more water if necessary to make the tamarind juice up to 250ml/8floz (1 cup). Discard the contents of the strainer.

Heat 50ml/2floz (¼ cup) of the oil in a saucepan. Add the okra and fry until they are golden brown. Transfer to a plate and set aside.

Add the onions, ginger, garlic and chillis to

Pakoras are tasty vegetable fritters which are very popular as a snack dish in India. In this particular recipe, cauliflower has been used but any type of vegetable can be substituted.

the pan and fry until the onions are golden brown. Add the turmeric and coriander and fry for 3 minutes, stirring constantly. Add a spoonful or two of water if the mixture becomes too dry.

Pour in the tamarind juice, return the okra to the pan and bring to the boil. Reduce the heat to low, cover the pan and simmer for 5 minutes. Stir in the coconut milk and salt, and bring to the boil again. Reduce the heat to low and simmer, uncovered, for 10 minutes.

Meanwhile, heat the remaining oil in a small frying-pan. Add the mustard seeds and curry or bay leaves. Cover the pan and fry until the seeds pop. Stir the contents of this pan into the okra mixture and cook for 1 minute.

Transfer the curry to a warmed serving dish and serve at once.

4 Servings

CURRIED POTATOES AND PEAS

This dish is eaten all over India, either on its own with chappati or puris, or as part of a meal.

	Metric/U.K.	U.S.
Ghee or vegetable oil	3 Tbs	3 Tbs
Medium onion, finely chopped	1	1
Fresh root ginger, peeled and finely chopped	2½cm/1in piece	1in piece
Garlic cloves, chopped	2	2
Green chilli, chopped	1	1
Turmeric	1 tsp	1 tsp
Frozen or fresh peas, thawed	½kg/1lb	1lb
Potatoes, cubed	225g/8oz	8oz
Salt	1 tsp	1 tsp
Chopped coriander leaves	2 Tbs	2 Tbs
Juice of ½ lemon		

Sabzi Kari is a filling, easy-to-make mixed vegetable curry.

Heat the ghee or oil in a saucepan. Add the onion and fry until it is soft. Stir in the ginger, garlic and chilli and cook for a further 5 minutes, stirring frequently. Stir in the turmeric, then the peas, potatoes and salt. Reduce the heat to low, cover the pan and simmer for 20 minutes. Add a spoonful or two of water if the mixture becomes too dry.

Stir in the coriander leaves and lemon juice, and simmer for a further 10 to 15 minutes, or until the vegetables are tender. Serve at once.

4 Servings

JUMPING POTATOES

This dish is an essential part of a special festive dish called Alu Makhala, a speciality of a small group of Middle Eastern Jews living in India. They can, of course, be served as an accompaniment to other Indian meat or vegetable dishes.

	Metric/U.K.	U.S.
Medium potatoes, peeled	1kg/2lb	2lb
Salt	1 tsp	1 tsp
Turmeric	½ tsp	½ tsp
Vegetable oil	950ml/32floz	4 cups

Put the potatoes into a large saucepan and barely cover them with cold water. Add the salt and turmeric and bring to the boil. Boil for 30 seconds, remove from the heat and drain the potatoes.

Heat the oil in a large deep-frying pan (one that is large enough to take the potatoes in one layer). When it is hot, but not hot enough to fry the potatoes, add the potatoes. Simmer for

10 to 15 minutes or until they begin to soften. (Test by prodding them with a fork.) Remove from the heat and let the potatoes cool in the oil.

Twenty minutes before serving, return the pan to high heat and heat the oil until it is very hot. When the potatoes float to the top continue cooking, stirring constantly, for 5 to 6 minutes, or until the potatoes are crisp and golden brown.

Run enough cold water into the sink to make a depth of about 5cm/2in. Remove the pan from the heat and place it in the water. Stir the potatoes gently for 2 minutes. Using a slotted spoon, remove the potatoes from the oil and arrange them on a warmed serving dish. Serve very hot.

4-6 Servings

SABZI KARI
(Vegetable Curry)

The vegetables given below are only suggestions— this delightful dish can be made with others, too.

	Metric/U.K.	U.S.
Vegetable oil	3 Tbs	3 Tbs
Medium onions, chopped	2	2
Fresh root ginger, peeled and finely chopped	4cm/1½in piece	1½in piece
Garlic cloves, crushed	2	2
Green chillis, chopped	2	2
Turmeric	1 tsp	1 tsp
Ground coriander	1 Tbs	1 Tbs
Paprika	1 Tbs	1 Tbs
Cayenne pepper	½ tsp	½ tsp
Ground fenugreek	¼ tsp	¼ tsp
Black pepper	¼ tsp	¼ tsp
Lemon juice	2 Tbs	2 Tbs
Potatoes, cubed	½kg/1lb	1lb
Turnip, cubed	1	1
Carrots, sliced	3	3
French beans, sliced	125g/4oz	⅔ cup
Fresh peas, weighed after shelling	125g/4oz	⅔ cup

There are over 60 varieties of lentil in India so it is almost inevitable that there are some superb Indian lentil dishes. Sambar (recipe on the following page) is a southern Indian speciality.

	Metric/U.K.	U.S.
Salt	1 tsp	1 tsp
Canned peeled tomatoes, rubbed through a strainer with the juice	425g/14oz	14oz

Heat the oil in a large saucepan. Add the onions, ginger, garlic and chillis and fry until the onions are golden brown.

Meanwhile, combine the turmeric, coriander, paprika, cayenne, fenugreek and pepper. Add the lemon juice and a little water, if necessary, to make a smooth paste. Add the spice paste to the onion mixture and fry for 5 minutes, stirring constantly. Add a spoonful or two of water if the mixture becomes too dry. Add the vegetables to the pan and fry for 5 minutes, stirring constantly. Stir in the salt and tomatoes and bring to the boil. Reduce the heat to low, cover the pan and simmer the curry for 25 minutes, or until the vegetables are tender.

Transfer the curry to a warmed serving dish and serve at once.

4-6 Servings

SAMBAR
(Lentils Cooked with Spices)

There are over sixty varieties of lentils to be found in India, and their popularity is what you might expect from a population that is, at least in theory, overwhelmingly vegetarian. This particular south Indian dish calls for toovar dhal (lentils) but any available type may be substituted.

	Metric/U.K.	U.S.
Toovar dhal (lentils), washed, soaked for 1 hour and drained	225g/8oz	1 cup
Ground fenugreek	$\frac{1}{2}$ tsp	$\frac{1}{2}$ tsp
Water	$1\frac{1}{4}$ 1/2 pints	5 cups
Salt	$1\frac{1}{2}$ tsp	$1\frac{1}{2}$ tsp
Fresh coconut, chopped	50g/2oz	$\frac{1}{3}$ cup
Whole cumin seeds	2 tsp	2 tsp
Coriander seeds	1 Tbs	1 Tbs
Ground cinnamon	$\frac{1}{2}$ tsp	$\frac{1}{2}$ tsp
Tamarind	50g/2oz	$\frac{1}{4}$ cup
Boiling water	250ml/8floz	1 cup
Soft brown sugar	2 tsp	2 tsp
Hot chilli powder	1 tsp	1 tsp
Chopped coriander leaves	2 Tbs	2 Tbs
Vegetable oil	2 Tbs	2 Tbs
Mustard seeds	1 tsp	1 tsp
Turmeric	1 tsp	1 tsp
Asafoetida (optional)	$\frac{1}{4}$ tsp	$\frac{1}{4}$ tsp
Garlic cloves, crushed	2	2
Green chilli, chopped	1	1

Put the dhal, fenugreek, water and 1 teaspoon of salt into a saucepan and bring to the boil. Reduce the heat to low and simmer for 1 hour, or until the dhal is soft. Remove from the heat.

Meanwhile, cook the coconut, cumin, coriander and cinnamon in a frying-pan, stirring constantly with a wooden spoon, for 3 minutes. Remove from the heat and allow the mixture to cool. Purée in a blender with 4 tablespoons of cold water, then transfer the mixture to a bowl and set aside.

Put the tamarind in a small bowl and pour over the boiling water. Set aside until the mixture is cool. Pour the mixture through a strainer into a saucepan, using the back of a wooden spoon to push through as much of the softened tamarind pulp as possible. Discard the contents of the strainer.

Put the saucepan over moderate heat. Stir in the sugar, chilli powder, coriander leaves and remaining salt and simmer the mixture for 5 minutes. Remove from the heat and set aside.

Heat the oil in a small frying-pan. Add the mustard seeds. Cover the pan and fry until they pop. Stir in the turmeric, asafoetida, if you are using it, the garlic and chilli. Reduce the heat to low and fry for 2 minutes, stirring constantly. Spoon the contents of the pan into the dhal with the tamarind mixture and coconut and spice purée. Return the pan to low heat and simmer the dhal mixture for 10 minutes, stirring frequently.

Remove from the heat and transfer to a warmed serving dish. Serve at once.

4 Servings

KHICHRI
(Rice with Lentils)

This is the dish from which evolved the Anglo-Indian breakfast dish of Kedgeree. It is usually served with spiced vegetables in India.

	Metric/U.K.	U.S.
Butter	75g/3oz	6 Tbs
Onion, finely chopped	1	1
Fresh root ginger, peeled and finely chopped	2½cm/1in piece	1in piece
Garlic clove, chopped	1	1
Peppercorns	6	6
Bay leaf	1	1
Long-grain rice, soaked in cold water for 1 hour and drained	225g/8oz	1⅓ cups
Moong dhal (yellow lentils), soaked with the rice in cold water for 1 hour and drained	125g/4oz	½ cup
Salt	1 tsp	1 tsp
Turmeric	½ tsp	½ tsp
Boiling water	600ml/1 pint	2½ cups

Fried onion rings
(to garnish)

Melt 50g/2oz (4 tablespoons) of the butter in a large saucepan. Add the onion and fry until it is soft. Stir in the ginger, garlic, peppercorns and bay leaf and fry for 3 minutes, stirring constantly.

Add the rice, dhal, salt and turmeric. Stir and toss the mixture gently. Reduce the heat to moderately low and continue cooking and stirring for 5 minutes. Pour in the boiling water and stir once. Reduce the heat to low, cover the pan and simmer for 15 to 20 minutes, or until the rice and dhal are cooked and the water has been absorbed. Stir in the remaining butter.

Turn the khichri into a warmed serving dish and scatter over the fried onion rings. Serve at once.

4 Servings

Rice with Aubergine (Eggplant) and Potatoes can be served either as an accompaniment to a meat or fish curry or, with other vegetable dishes, as a light meal.

Pulao with Cashew Nuts makes a delightful accompaniment to meat or poultry dishes. Scatter over some blanched almonds for a particularly effective garnish.

RICE WITH AUBERGINE (EGGPLANT) AND POTATOES

	Metric/U.K.	U.S.
Long-grain rice, soaked in cold water for 30 minutes and drained	275g/10oz	1⅔ cups
Water	600ml/1 pint	2½ cups
Salt	1½ tsp	1½ tsp
Turmeric	1 tsp	1 tsp
Ground cumin	1 tsp	1 tsp
Ground coriander	1 Tbs	1 Tbs
Cayenne pepper	½ tsp	½ tsp
Sugar	½ tsp	½ tsp
Lemon juice	1 Tbs	1 Tbs
Chick-pea flour	2 tsp	2 tsp
Ghee or clarified butter	50g/2oz	4 Tbs
Potatoes, cubed	350g/12oz	12oz
Aubergine (eggplant), cubed and dégorged	1	1
Butter, melted	50g/2oz	4 Tbs

Put the rice into a large saucepan. Pour over the water and 1 teaspoon of salt. Bring to the boil. Cover the pan and simmer for 15 to 20 minutes, or until the rice is tender and the water has been absorbed. Remove from the heat, set aside and keep warm.

Meanwhile, combine the turmeric, cumin, coriander, cayenne, sugar, lemon juice, flour and remaining salt to a paste, adding more lemon juice if necessary. Set aside.

Preheat the oven to moderate 180°C (Gas Mark 4, 350°F).

Melt the ghee or clarified butter in a large frying-pan. Add the potato and aubergine (eggplant) cubes and fry for 10 minutes, stirring constantly. Add a spoonful or two of water if the mixture becomes too dry. Reduce the heat to low, cover the pan and simmer for 15 to 20 minutes, or until the vegetables are tender. Set aside.

Spread half the rice over the bottom of an ovenproof dish. Sprinkle 25g/1oz (2 table-spoons) of the melted butter over the rice. Spread the vegetable mixture over the rice and cover with the remaining rice. Sprinkle the remaining melted butter over the top. Cover and put the dish into the oven. Cook for 25 minutes.

Remove from the oven and serve immediately.

4 Servings

PULAU WITH CASHEW NUTS

This dish is filling enough to constitute a light meal on its own (with, perhaps, some poppadums), or it makes a filling accompaniment to meat or fish.

	Metric/U.K.	U.S.
Butter	75g/3oz	6 Tbs
Small pineapple, peeled, cored and cut into chunks	1	1
Raisins	3 Tbs	3 Tbs
Spring onions (scallions), chopped	12	12
Unsalted cashew nuts	75g/3oz	½ cup
Coriander seeds, crushed	1 Tbs	1 Tbs
Cayenne pepper	¼ tsp	¼ tsp
Long-grain rice, soaked in cold water for 30 minutes and drained	350g/12oz	2 cups
Salt	1 tsp	1 tsp
Chicken stock	600ml/1 pint	2½ cups
Hard-boiled eggs, quartered	2	2
Chopped coriander leaves	1 Tbs	1 Tbs

Melt half the butter in a frying-pan. Add the pineapple chunks and raisins and fry until the pineapple is lightly browned. Remove the pan from the heat and set aside.

Melt the remaining butter in a large saucepan. Add the spring onions (scallions) and fry until they are golden brown. Stir in the cashew nuts, coriander seeds and cayenne and fry for 4 minutes, stirring occasionally. Stir in the rice and salt and fry for 5 minutes, stirring constantly. Stir in the pineapple mixture, then pour over the stock and bring to the boil. Reduce the heat to low, cover the pan and simmer for 20 to 25 minutes, or until the rice is tender and the liquid has been absorbed.

Transfer the pulau to a warmed serving dish, sprinkle over the coriander.

Serve at once.

4 Servings

EKURI
(Scrambled Eggs with Chilli)

This is one of the eating delights of the Parsees, a religious community in western India.

	Metric/U.K.	U.S.
Butter	40g/1½oz	3 Tbs
Medium onion, finely chopped	1	1
Fresh root ginger, peeled and finely chopped	1cm/½in piece	½in piece
Green chilli, finely chopped	1	1
Turmeric	½ tsp	½ tsp
Chopped coriander leaves	2 Tbs	2 Tbs
Salt	½ tsp	½ tsp
Eggs, lightly beaten	8	8
Bread, slightly toasted	4 slices	4 slices
Tomatoes, quartered	2	2

Melt the butter in a medium frying-pan. Add the onion and ginger and fry until the onion is soft. Stir in the chilli, turmeric, 1½ tablespoons of coriander leaves and salt and fry for 1 minute.

Pour in the beaten eggs, reduce the heat to low and cook the eggs until they are softly scrambled, stirring constantly.

Spoon the mixture on to the toast, garnish with the tomato quarters and remaining coriander leaves.

Serve at once.

4 Servings

Meat

KOFTA KARI
(Meatball Curry)

These small spicy meatballs are served in a hot sauce (the original meaning of kari, or curry, was sauce). Although this version is made with minced (ground) beef, lamb may be substituted if you prefer.

	Metric/U.K.	U.S.
MEATBALLS		
Minced (ground) beef	700g/1½lb	1½lb
Chick-pea flour	3 Tbs	3 Tbs
Fresh root ginger, peeled and chopped	1cm/½in piece	½in piece
Garlic cloves, crushed	2	2
Hot chilli powder	½ tsp	½ tsp
Salt	1 tsp	1 tsp
Egg	1	1
Turmeric	½ tsp	½ tsp
Juice and finely grated rind of ½ lemon		
Onion, finely chopped	1	1
Vegetable oil	50ml/2floz	¼ cup
SAUCE		
Vegetable oil	2 Tbs	2 Tbs
Onions, finely chopped	2	2
Fresh root ginger, peeled and chopped	1cm/½in piece	½in piece
Garlic cloves, crushed	2	2
Green chillis, chopped	2	2
Turmeric	1 tsp	1 tsp
Ground coriander	1 Tbs	1 Tbs
Ground cumin	1 tsp	1 tsp
Paprika	2 tsp	2 tsp
Creamed coconut	2½cm/1in slice	1in slice
Boiling water	450ml/15floz	2 cups
Curry leaves (optional)	3	3
Salt	1 tsp	1 tsp

First, make the meatballs. Put all the ingredients, except the oil, in a bowl and, using your hands, knead well to blend. Shape the mixture into about 24 small balls.

Heat the oil in a large frying-pan. Add the meatballs and fry until they are golden brown all over. (Don't crowd the pan; if necessary fry the balls in two or three batches.) Transfer the meatballs to a plate as they brown.

To make the sauce, heat the oil in a large saucepan. Add the onions and fry until they are golden brown. Stir in the ginger, garlic and chillis, and fry for 3 minutes. Stir in the turmeric, coriander, cumin and paprika and fry for 5 minutes. Add a spoonful or two of water if the mixture becomes too dry.

Meanwhile, dissolve the creamed coconut in the water, then stir into the saucepan with the curry leaves, if you are using them, and salt. Bring to the boil and reduce the heat to low. Cover and simmer the sauce for 15 minutes.

Add the meatballs to the pan, turning them over gently in the sauce to coat them well. Bring to the boil again. Reduce the heat to low, re-cover the pan and simmer for a further 20 minutes.

Remove from the heat and transfer the mixture to a warmed serving dish. Serve at once.

4 Servings

KHEEMA
(Curried Minced [Ground] Meat)

This dish is often combined with peas or cabbage in India to provide a light main dish. If you prefer a mild curry, reduce the amount of chilli powder.

	Metric/U.K.	U.S.
Vegetable oil	50ml/2floz	¼ cup
Medium onions, thinly sliced	4	4
Fresh root ginger, peeled and finely chopped	2½cm/1in piece	1in piece
Garlic cloves, crushed	2	2
Turmeric	1 tsp	1 tsp
Hot chilli powder	1 tsp	1 tsp
Ground coriander	1 tsp	1 tsp
Minced (ground) beef	700g/1½lb	1½lb
Salt	½ tsp	½ tsp
Tomatoes, blanched, peeled and chopped	3	3

Chopped coriander leaves	2 Tbs	2 Tbs

Heat the oil in a saucepan. Add the onions, ginger and garlic and fry until the onions are soft. Stir in the turmeric, chilli powder and coriander, and fry for 3 minutes, stirring constantly. Stir in the meat and fry until it is well browned. Add the salt and tomatoes. Stir well, reduce the heat to moderately low and cover the pan. Simmer the kheema for 10 minutes.

Uncover the pan and cook for a further 5 minutes. Adjust seasoning and serve at once.

4 Servings

DRY BEEF CURRY

This is a very basic and easy-to-make dish. If you wish it to be less pungent, seed the chillis before cooking them. Serve with plain rice and a selection of raitas, sambals and chutney.

	Metric/U.K.	U.S.
Vegetable oil	50ml/2floz	$\frac{1}{4}$ cup
Green chillis, chopped	2	2
Medium onions, chopped	2	2
Stewing or chuck steak, cubed	1kg/2lb	2lb
Salt	$\frac{1}{2}$ tsp	$\frac{1}{2}$ tsp
Tomatoes, blanched, peeled and chopped	2	2
Turmeric	1 tsp	1 tsp
Ground cumin	1 tsp	1 tsp
Ground coriander	2 tsp	2 tsp
Garam masala	$1\frac{1}{2}$ tsp	$1\frac{1}{2}$ tsp
Yogurt	300ml/10floz	$1\frac{1}{4}$ cups
Chopped coriander leaves	1 Tbs	1 Tbs

Heat the oil in a saucepan. Add the chillis and fry for 1 minute. Stir in the onions and fry until they are golden brown. Add the beef cubes and salt. Fry for 10 to 15 minutes, or until they are deeply browned all over. Stir in the tomatoes and cook for 10 minutes, or until most of the liquid has evaporated.

Combine the turmeric, cumin, coriander and 1 teaspoon of the garam masala. Beat in the yogurt. Stir this mixture into the mixture in the pan, reduce the heat to low and half-cover. Simmer for $1\frac{1}{2}$ hours.

Remove the lid from the pan and simmer the curry for a further 30 minutes, or until the liquid has evaporated leaving the meat covered in a thick gravy. If the curry becomes too dry too quickly, cover and continue cooking.

Transfer the mixture to a warmed serving dish and sprinkle over the remaining garam masala and the coriander leaves.

Serve at once.

4-6 Servings

Kofta Kari are savoury little meatballs covered with a hot, spicy sauce.

GOSHT AUR ALOO
(Beef and Potato Curry)

	Metric/U.K.	U.S.
Ghee or clarified butter	50g/2oz	4 Tbs
Onions, finely chopped	2	2
Garlic clove, crushed	1	1
Fresh root ginger, peeled and chopped	4cm/1½in piece	1½in piece
Green chillis, chopped	2	2
Turmeric	1 tsp	1 tsp
Ground coriander	1 Tbs	1 Tbs
Hot chilli powder	¼ tsp	¼ tsp
Ground cumin	1 tsp	1 tsp
Cardamom seeds, crushed	1 Tbs	1 Tbs
Ground cloves	½ tsp	½ tsp
Lean stewing or chuck steak, cubed	1kg/2lb	2lb
Water	450ml/15floz	2 cups
Salt	1 tsp	1 tsp
Bay leaves	2	2
Small potatoes, scrubbed	½kg/1lb	1lb

Melt the ghee or butter in a large saucepan. Add the onions and garlic and fry until they are golden brown. Stir in the ginger and chillis and fry for 4 minutes. Stir in the turmeric, coriander, chilli powder, cumin, cardamom and cloves and fry for 6 minutes, stirring frequently. Add a spoonful or two of water if the mixture becomes too dry.

Add the meat cubes and fry until they are evenly browned. Stir in the water, salt and bay leaves, and bring to the boil. When the mixture begins to bubble, reduce the heat to low and simmer for 1¼ hours.

Add the potatoes and bring to the boil again. Cover and simmer for a further 45 minutes, or until the meat is cooked through and tender. Taste and add more salt if necessary.

Transfer the mixture to a warmed serving dish and serve at once.

4-6 Servings

TURKARI MOLEE
(Lamb and Coconut Curry)

A molee in Indian cooking is a curry in which coconut is used as one of the main flavourings. This is one of the basic molees.

	Metric/U.K.	U.S.
Ghee or clarified butter	50g/2oz	4 Tbs
Medium onions, sliced	2	2
Garlic cloves, crushed	6	6
Fresh root ginger, peeled and finely chopped	5cm/2in piece	2in piece
Turmeric	1½ tsp	1½ tsp
Hot chilli powder	2 tsp	2 tsp
Black pepper	½ tsp	½ tsp
Ground fenugreek	½ tsp	½ tsp
Ground coriander	2 tsp	2 tsp
Ground cumin	1 tsp	1 tsp
Paprika	2 tsp	2 tsp
Lean lamb, cubed	1kg/2lb	2lb
Coconut milk	600ml/1 pint	2½ cups
Salt	1½ tsp	1½ tsp
Curry leaves (optional)	2	2

Melt the ghee or clarified butter in a large saucepan. Add the onions and fry until they are golden brown. Add the garlic, ginger, turmeric, chilli powder, pepper, fenugreek, coriander, cumin and paprika and fry for 5 minutes, stirring constantly. Add a spoonful or two of water if the mixture becomes too dry.

Add the lamb cubes and fry for 10 minutes, turning them frequently. Pour in the coconut milk and add the salt and curry leaves, if you are using them. Bring to the boil. Reduce the heat to low, cover the pan and simmer for 1 hour or until the lamb is cooked through and tender.

Transfer to a warmed serving dish and serve at once.

4-6 Servings

KABAB MASSALAM
(Minced [Ground] Lamb kebabs)

These spicy cigar-shaped kebabs are popular all over India. The thick wooden skewers tradi-tionally used for kebabs in India should be used in this dish—the mixture adheres to it better than it would to a metal skewer. Serve on a bed of rice, or over bread as in the picture overleaf and a selection of chutneys.

Succulent beef and small new potatoes form the basis of this unusual dish, called Gosht aur Aloo.

kebabs for 5 minutes. Turn, then brush with the remaining melted butter and grill (broil) for a further 5 minutes, or until the kebabs are cooked through.

Arrange the skewers on a warmed serving dish and garnish with the lemon quarters. Serve at once.

4 Servings

ZEERA GOSHT
(Cumin Lamb)

In Indian cooking, the masala, or combination of spices, is usually such that no one spice 'stands out' in the finished dish—but occasionally, to provide a different taste for a dish, one is allowed to predominate. The 'zeera' in this succulent lamb dish means that the singled-out taste is cumin.

The Indians are very fond of kebabs and they are cooked in many different ways. This particular Kabab Massalam is simply minced (ground) meat wrapped around traditional thick wooden skewers and grilled (broiled). The result is absolutely delicious.

	Metric/U.K.	U.S.
Garlic cloves, crushed	3	3
Fresh root ginger, peeled and finely chopped	4cm/1½in piece	1½in piece
Green chillis, finely chopped	2	2
Medium onion, chopped	1	1
Chopped coriander leaves	2 Tbs	2 Tbs
Yogurt	3 Tbs	3 Tbs
Turmeric	½ tsp	½ tsp
Lemon juice	1 Tbs	1 Tbs
Salt	1 tsp	1 tsp
Fresh breadcrumbs	15g/½oz	¼ cup
Minced (ground) lamb	700g/1½lb	1½lb
Butter, melted	25g/1oz	2 Tbs
Lemons, quartered	2	2

Combine all the ingredients, except the melted butter and lemons, in a large bowl. Using your hands, lightly knead until the ingredients are blended and the mixture is stiff. Cover and set aside to 'rest' for 30 minutes.

Preheat the grill (broiler) to high. Lightly grease 12 skewers with a little of the melted butter. With dampened hands, remove small pieces of the meat mixture and shape them into cigar shapes around the skewers, two to a skewer.

Lay the skewers on the lined grill (broiler) pan and brush them with about half the remaining melted butter. Grill (broil) the

	Metric/U.K.	U.S.
Whole cumin seeds	1 Tbs	1 Tbs
Fresh root ginger, peeled and chopped	2½cm/1in piece	1in piece
Garlic cloves	3	3
Cardamom seeds	2 tsp	2 tsp
Whole cloves	2	2
Blanched almonds	12	12
Sesame seeds	2 tsp	2 tsp
Cayenne pepper	1 tsp	1 tsp
Salt	1 tsp	1 tsp
Soft brown sugar	1 tsp	1 tsp
Yogurt	175ml/6floz	¾ cup
Butter	40g/1½oz	3 Tbs
Medium onion, finely chopped	1	1
Large green or red peppers, pith and seeds removed and sliced	2	2
Boned leg of lamb, cubed	1kg/2lb	2lb
Ground saffron	¼ tsp	¼ tsp

Put the cumin seeds, ginger, garlic, cardamom seeds, cloves, almonds, sesame seeds, cayenne, salt, sugar and 2 tablespoons of the yogurt into a blender and blend to a purée, adding more yogurt if the mixture becomes too dry. Transfer the mixture to a small bowl and set aside.

Melt the butter in a large flameproof casserole. Add the onion and fry until it is golden brown. Stir in the spice paste and fry for 5 minutes, stirring constantly, adding a spoonful or two of water if the mixture becomes too dry. Add the peppers and fry for 2 minutes. Add the lamb and fry for 10 minutes, turning the cubes frequently.

Meanwhile, beat the remaining yogurt and saffron together, then pour the mixture into the casserole and mix well. Bring to the boil, reduce the heat to very low and cover the casserole. Simmer for 50 minutes.

Meanwhile, preheat the oven to cool 150°C (Gas Mark 2, 300°F).

Transfer the casserole to the oven and cook the lamb for 25 minutes. Remove from the oven and serve at once.

4-6 Servings

SAG GOSHT
(Lamb and Spinach Curry)

You can substitute lean veal cubes for the lamb in this dish, if you prefer.

	Metric/U.K.	U.S.
Ghee or clarified butter	50g/2oz	4 Tbs
Mustard seeds	1½ tsp	1½ tsp
Garlic cloves, crushed	2	2
Cardamom seeds, crushed	2 tsp	2 tsp
Ground coriander	1 Tbs	1 Tbs
Fresh root ginger, peeled and chopped	4cm/1½in piece	1½in piece
Lean boned lamb, cubed	1kg/2lb	2lb
Medium onion, chopped	1	1
Green chillis, chopped	3	3
Sugar	1 tsp	1 tsp
Turmeric	1 tsp	1 tsp
Spinach, trimmed, washed and chopped	1kg/2lb	2lb
Salt	1½ tsp	1½ tsp
Black pepper	½ tsp	½ tsp
Yogurt	3 Tbs	3 Tbs

Melt the ghee or butter in a flameproof casserole. Add the mustard seeds and cover.

Sag Gosht is a nutrious— and delicious—mixture of lean lamb cubes and velvety leaf spinach cooked together in a yogurt-based sauce.

Fry until the seeds begin to pop. Stir in the garlic, cardamom, coriander and ginger and fry for 1 minute, stirring constantly. Add the lamb cubes and fry until they are evenly browned.

Stir in the onion, chillis and sugar and fry until the onion is golden brown. Stir in the turmeric and spinach and cook for 3 minutes. Add the remaining ingredients and reduce the heat to low. Cover and simmer for 1 hour, or until the meat is cooked through and tender and the spinach is smooth and soft. Uncover and stir well.

Preheat the oven to cool 150°C (Gas Mark 2, 300°F). Put the casserole into the oven and cook for 20 minutes. Remove from the oven and serve at once.

4-6 Servings

ROGHAN JOSH
(Spiced Lamb)

This dish is one of the classics of Kashmiri cooking, although it is now eaten all over northern India. It is traditionally eaten with chappati or naan, rather than rice.

	Metric/U.K.	U.S.
Yogurt	250ml/8floz	1 cup
Asafoetida (optional)	¼ tsp	¼ tsp
Cayenne pepper	½ tsp	½ tsp
Boned leg of lamb, cubed	1kg/2lb	2lb
Fresh root ginger, peeled and chopped	4cm/1½in piece	1½in piece
Garlic cloves	4	4
White poppy seeds	1 tsp	1 tsp
Cumin seeds	1 tsp	1 tsp
Coriander seeds	1 Tbs	1 Tbs
Cloves	4	4
Cardamom seeds	1 Tbs	1 Tbs
Peppercorns	8	8
Whole unblanched almonds	2 Tbs	2 Tbs
Ghee or clarified butter	50g/2oz	4 Tbs
Medium onion, chopped	1	1
Turmeric	1 tsp	1 tsp
Water	250ml/8floz	1 cup
Garam masala	1 tsp	1 tsp
Chopped coriander leaves	1 Tbs	1 Tbs

Combine the yogurt, asafoetida, if you are using it, and cayenne in a large bowl. Add the lamb cubes, baste well, cover and set aside.

Put the ginger, garlic, poppy, cumin and coriander seeds, cloves, cardamom, peppercorns and almonds in a blender with 4 tablespoons of water and blend until the mixture forms a smooth paste. Add more water if necessary. Transfer the mixture to a small bowl and set aside.

Melt the ghee or clarified butter in a flameproof casserole. Add the onion and fry until it is golden brown. Stir in the turmeric and spice paste and fry for 8 minutes, stirring constantly. Add a spoonful or two of water if the mixture becomes too dry.

Increase the heat to high. Add the lamb cubes and marinade and fry for 10 minutes, stirring constantly. Reduce the heat to very low, cover and simmer for 45 minutes.

Uncover the casserole, increase the heat to moderate and stir in 50ml/2floz (¼ cup) of water until it has been absorbed. Add another 50ml/2floz (¼ cup) and stir until it has been absorbed. Pour in the remaining water, re-cover and simmer the lamb for a further 15 minutes.

Preheat the oven to very cool 140°C (Gas Mark 1, 275°F).

Stir in the garam masala and coriander leaves. Cover and put the casserole into the oven. Cook for 25 minutes. Remove from the oven, transfer the mixture to a warmed serving dish and serve at once.

4-6 Servings

SHAKOOTI RASSA
(Lamb Cooked with Coconut)

This spicy dish of lamb with vegetables comes from the west coast of India.

	Metric/U.K.	U.S.
Chillis, seeded	6	6
Chopped coriander leaves	6 Tbs	6 Tbs
Garlic cloves	3	3
Fresh root ginger, peeled and chopped	5cm/2in piece	2in piece

Salt	1 tsp	1 tsp	White poppy seeds	1 Tbs	1 Tbs
Thick coconut milk	475ml/16floz	2 cups	Black peppercorns	1 tsp	1 tsp
Boned leg of lamb, cubed	1kg/2lb	2lb	Turmeric	1 tsp	1 tsp
			Grated nutmeg	½ tsp	½ tsp
Ghee or clarified butter	65g/2½oz	5 Tbs	Medium onions, chopped	2	2
Fresh coconut, grated	½	½			
Whole cumin seeds	1 Tbs	1 Tbs	Potatoes, cubed	.½kg/1lb	1lb

Lamb and vegetables cooked with coconut, Shakooti Rassa is a western Indian speciality.

21

Raan is a classic Indian dish in which leg of lamb is marinated in yogurt and spices for 48 hours before being roasted until it is so tender the meat almost falls off the bones.

Put the chillis, coriander leaves, garlic, ginger and salt into a blender and blend, adding 2 to 3 tablespoons of coconut milk, to make a smooth paste. Alternatively, pound the ingredients in a mortar with a pestle. Transfer the spice paste to a large mixing bowl and add the meat cubes. Mix well, then set aside to marinate at room temperature for 6 hours, basting occasionally.

Melt 25g/1oz (2 tablespoons) of the ghee or clarified butter in a frying-pan. Add the grated coconut, cumin and poppy seeds, peppercorns, turmeric and nutmeg and fry, stirring constantly, for 5 minutes or until the ingredients are lightly browned. Remove from the heat and set aside to cool. When cool, put the mixture into the blender with 125ml/4floz ($\frac{1}{2}$ cup) of the remaining coconut milk and blend until it forms a smooth purée. Alternatively, pound in a mortar with a pestle. Set aside.

Melt the remaining ghee or clarified butter in a saucepan. Add the onions and fry until they are golden brown. Stir in the coconut and spice purée and fry for 5 minutes, stirring constantly. Stir in the meat mixture and fry for 10 minutes, or until the cubes are evenly browned. Pour in the remaining coconut milk, stir well and bring to the boil. Reduce the heat to low, cover the pan and simmer for 40 minutes.

Add the potatoes and more salt if necessary. Continue cooking, uncovered, for 20 minutes, or until the potatoes are tender and the sauce has thickened. Remove from the heat and transfer the shakooti to a warmed serving dish. Serve at once.

4-6 Servings

KORMA
(Lamb and Almond Curry)

Korma is a method of cooking in India, akin to braising in western cuisine. In this particular basic korma the braising agents are yogurt and cream, although stock and even water are sometimes used. Kormas can be made with most kinds of meat and vegetables.

	Metric/U.K.	U.S.
Medium onions, chopped	2	2
Fresh root ginger, peeled and chopped	4cm/1½in piece	1½in piece
Garlic cloves, crushed	3	3
Ground saffron	½ tsp	½ tsp
Yogurt	150ml/5floz	⅝ cup
Boned leg of lamb, cut into cubes	1kg/2lb	2lb
Butter	50g/2oz	4 Tbs
Hot chilli powder	½ tsp	½ tsp
Dill seed, crushed	1 tsp	1 tsp
Salt	1 tsp	1 tsp
Ground almonds	50g/2oz	⅓ cup
Double (heavy) cream	150ml/5floz	⅝ cup

Combine half the onions, half the ginger, half the garlic, the saffron and 2 to 3 tablespoons of yogurt in a large bowl. Add the meat and baste well. Set aside to marinate for 1 hour.

Melt the butter in a large saucepan. Add the remaining onions, ginger and garlic and fry until they are deep golden brown. Using a slotted spoon, transfer the mixture to a plate.

Add the meat mixture to the pan and fry until they are evenly browned. Moisten the meat with a spoonful or two of yogurt while frying. As it dries, add more yogurt. Stir in the onion mixture, chilli powder, dill, salt and any remaining yogurt. Reduce the heat to low and simmer the meat, stirring occasionally, for 40 minutes. Add a spoonful or two of water if the mixture becomes too dry.

Mix the almonds and cream together, then stir the mixture into the lamb. Cover the pan and continue to simmer the korma for a further 15 to 20 minutes, or until the lamb is cooked through and tender.

Transfer to a warmed serving dish and serve at once.

4-6 Servings

RAAN
(Leg of Lamb Marinated in Spiced Yogurt and Roasted)

	Metric/U.K.	U.S.
Leg of lamb, trimmed of fat	1x3kg/6lb	1x6lb
Fresh root ginger, peeled and chopped	125g/4oz	4oz
Large garlic cloves, peeled	12	12
Thinly pared rind of 1 lemon		
Lemon juice	5 Tbs	5 Tbs
Cumin seeds	2 tsp	2 tsp
Cardamom seeds	1 Tbs	1 Tbs
Whole cloves	8	8
Turmeric	1 tsp	1 tsp
Hot chilli powder	1½ tsp	1½ tsp
Salt	1 Tbs	1 Tbs
Unblanched almonds	150g/5oz	1 cup
Soft brown sugar	4 Tbs	4 Tbs
Yogurt	300ml/10floz	1¼ cups
Saffron threads, soaked in 2 Tbs boiling water	½ tsp	½ tsp

Prick the leg of lamb all over. Make several deep gashes in the flesh, then transfer to a large, deep roasting pan. Set aside.

Put the ginger, garlic, lemon rind and juice, cumin seeds, cardamom seeds, cloves, turmeric, chilli powder and salt in a blender and blend to a purée. Scrape the purée out of the blender and spread it all over the lamb. Set aside for 1 hour.

Put the almonds, 2 tablespoons of the sugar and half the yogurt into the blender and blend until they form a purée. Transfer to a small bowl and stir in the remaining yogurt. Spread this mixture all over the lamb, on top of the spice purée. Cover the pan and chill in the refrigerator for 48 hours.

Preheat the oven to hot 220°C (Gas Mark 7, 425°F).

Remove the pan from the refrigerator and allow the lamb to warm to room temperature. Sprinkle over the remaining sugar. Put the pan into the oven and roast for 20 minutes. Reduce the oven temperature to moderate 180°C (Gas Mark 4, 350°F) and roast for a further 1 hour. Reduce the temperature to warm 170°C (Gas Mark 3, 325°F), cover the pan and roast, basting occasionally, for 4 hours.

Remove from the oven and, using two large forks or spoons, transfer the lamb to a large piece of foil. Cover the meat completely and return to the oven.

Remove any excess fat from the pan, then stir in the saffron mixture. Place the pan over high heat and boil the sauce rapidly for 15 to 20 minutes, or until it is reduced by half. Remove from the heat.

Remove the lamb from the oven and discard the foil. Arrange on a warmed serving dish, spoon over the sauce and serve at once.

8-10 Servings

TALAWA GOSHT
(Deep-Fried Lamb and Potatoes)

	Metric/U.K.	U.S.
Butter	25g/1oz	2 Tbs
Fresh root ginger, peeled and finely chopped	4cm/1½in piece	1½in piece
Garlic cloves, crushed	3	3
Boned leg of lamb, cubed	700g/1½lb	1½lb
Turmeric	1 tsp	1 tsp
Hot chilli powder	2 tsp	2 tsp
Salt	½ tsp	½ tsp
Yogurt	50ml/2floz	¼ cup

	Metric/U.K.	U.S.
Sufficient vegetable oil for deep-frying		
Potatoes, boiled until nearly tender, drained and cubed	½kg/1lb	1lb
Lemons, cut into wedges	2	2
BATTER		
Chick-pea flour	225g/8oz	2 cups
Salt	1 tsp	1 tsp
Hot chilli powder	½ tsp	½ tsp
Yogurt	75ml/3floz	⅜ cup
Water	250ml/8floz	1 cup

Melt the butter in a deep frying-pan. Add the ginger and garlic and fry for 3 minutes, stirring frequently. Add the meat cubes and fry until they are evenly browned.

Meanwhile, combine the turmeric, chilli powder, salt and yogurt together in a small bowl. Stir the mixture into the pan and cook, uncovered, for 30 minutes or until the lamb is just cooked through. Set aside to cool.

To make the batter, sift the flour, salt and chilli powder into a large bowl. Beat in the yogurt and stir in the water, a little at a time, until the mixture forms a smooth batter. Set aside for 30 minutes.

Fill a deep-frying pan one-third full with oil and heat until it reaches 185°C (360°F) on a deep-fat thermometer, or until a small cube of stale bread dropped into the oil turns golden in 50 seconds. Dip the lamb and potato cubes into the batter, then carefully lower them, a few at a time, into the hot oil. Fry for 3 to 4 minutes, or until they are golden brown and crisp. Remove from the oil and drain on kitchen towels.

Serve at once, garnished with the lemon wedges.

4 Servings

BADAMI GOSHT
(Lamb with Almonds)

	Metric/U.K.	U.S.
Ghee or clarified butter	65g/2½oz	5 Tbs
Cinnamon sticks	2x10cm/4in	2x4in
Whole cloves	6	6
Cardamom seeds	1 Tbs	1 Tbs
Large onion, chopped	1	1
Garlic cloves, crushed	2	2

Fresh root ginger, peeled and finely chopped	4cm/1½in piece	1½in piece
Boned leg of lamb, cubed	700g/1½lb	1½lb
Yogurt	300ml/10floz	1¼ cups
Saffron threads, soaked in 2 Tbs boiling water	1 tsp	1 tsp
Hot chilli powder	½ tsp	½ tsp
Ground almonds	75g/3oz	½ cup
Salt	1 tsp	1 tsp
Coconut milk	350ml/12floz	1½ cups
Dried red chillis	2	2

Melt the ghee or butter in a saucepan. Add the cinnamon, cloves and cardamom seeds and fry for 1 minute, stirring constantly. Add the onion and fry until it is soft. Add the garlic and ginger and fry for 2 minutes, stirring constantly. Add the lamb cubes to the pan and fry until they are evenly browned.

Combine the yogurt, saffron mixture and chilli powder in a small bowl, beating to blend thoroughly. In a second bowl, combine the almonds with enough water to make a smooth paste.

Stir the yogurt mixture and almond paste into the lamb cubes, then stir in the salt. Simmer the mixture for 15 minutes. Stir in the coconut milk and red chillis, and simmer for a further 40 minutes, or until the lamb is cooked through and tender. Cover the lamb for the last 10 minutes of cooking.

Serve at once.

4 Servings

Almonds and coconut form the flavourful base of this lamb curry known as Badami Gosht.

YAKHNI PULAO
(Lamb Cooked with Rice)

Yakhni in Indian cooking is similar to a western stock and is used as a basis for many dishes. The stock can be made with almost any type of meat or poultry, although lamb, as here, and chicken are the most popular.

Yakhni in India is a type of highly flavoured stock, and in this dish it is cooked with lean lamb cubes and rice to make a superb Yakhni Pulao.

	Metric/U.K.	U.S.
Boned leg of lamb, cubed and with the bones reserved	1kg/2lb	2lb
Pared rind of 1 lemon		
Fresh root ginger, peeled and thinly sliced	1cm/½in piece	½in piece
Cinnamon stick, bruised	2x5cm/2in pieces	2x2in pieces
Grated nutmeg	¼ tsp	¼ tsp
Green chilli, chopped	1	1
Black peppercorns	12	12
Yogurt	150ml/5floz	⅝ cup
Cayenne pepper	½ tsp	½ tsp
Juice of ½ lemon		
Salt	1½ tsp	1½ tsp
Butter	125g/4oz	8 Tbs
Medium onion, finely chopped	1	1
Whole cloves, bruised	4	4
Cardamom seeds, bruised	4	4
Whole cumin seeds	1 tsp	1 tsp
Long-grain rice, soaked in cold water for 30 minutes and drained	350g/12oz	2 cups
GARNISH Slivered almonds, lightly toasted	2 Tbs	2 Tbs

	Metric/U.K.	U.S.
Medium onion, thinly sliced and fried until golden	1	1
Raisins, lightly fried	2 Tbs	2 Tbs
Hard-boiled eggs, quartered	2	2

Put the lamb, the reserved bones, lemon rind, ginger, cinnamon, nutmeg, chilli and peppercorns in a large saucepan. Add enough water to cover the lamb and bones generously and bring to the boil. Reduce the heat to low, cover and simmer the mixture for 40 minutes, or until the lamb cubes are cooked through and tender.

Using a slotted spoon, transfer the lamb cubes to a bowl. Re-cover the pan and continue simmering the stock for 2 hours. Remove from the heat and strain into a bowl, discarding the contents of the strainer. Set the stock aside to cool. When it is cold, skim off and discard the fat on the surface.

Meanwhile, combine the yogurt, cayenne, lemon juice and half the salt. Pour the mixture over the lamb cubes and coat well. Cover the bowl and set aside for 2 hours.

Melt half the butter in a large saucepan. Add the onion and fry until it is golden brown. Stir in the cloves, cardamom and cumin and fry for 2 minutes. Stir in the rice and fry for 6 to 8 minutes, or until the rice becomes translucent.

Preheat the oven to very cool 140°C (Gas Mark 1, 275°F).

Meanwhile, pour the stock into a saucepan and bring to the boil. Remove from the heat and pour the stock over the rice, to cover it by about 1cm/½in. Add the remaining salt and, when the mixture comes back to the boil, reduce the heat to low and cover the pan. Simmer for 15 to 20 minutes, or until the rice is tender and the stock has been absorbed. Remove from the heat.

Meanwhile, melt the remaining butter in a frying-pan. Add the lamb cubes and marinade and fry for 5 minutes, stirring constantly. Reduce the heat to low and simmer for 10 minutes, stirring frequently. Remove from the heat.

Layer the rice and lamb into a large baking dish, beginning and ending with a layer of rice. Cover tightly with foil. Put the dish into the oven and bake for 20 minutes.

Combine the almonds, onion and raisins together and set aside.

Remove the dish from the oven and sprinkle over the garnish and eggs.

4-6 Servings

BOTI KEBABS
(Lamb on Skewers)

This is one of the basic tandoori dishes—dishes cooked in the clay oven called tandoor.

	Metric/U.K.	U.S.
Boned leg of lamb, cubed	1kg/2lb	2lb
Yogurt	150ml/5floz	⅝ cup
Ground coriander	1 Tbs	1 Tbs
Turmeric	1 tsp	1 tsp
Hot chilli powder	½ tsp	½ tsp
Salt	1 tsp	1 tsp
Garlic cloves, crushed	2	2
Fresh root ginger, peeled and finely chopped	2½cm/1in piece	1in piece
Chopped coriander leaves	1 Tbs	1 Tbs
Lemons, cut into wedges	2	2

Put the lamb cubes into a large bowl. Combine the yogurt, coriander, turmeric, chilli powder, salt, garlic and ginger and beat well. Pour over the lamb cubes, baste well and cover the bowl. Chill in the refrigerator for 6 hours, or overnight, basting occasionally.

Preheat the grill (broiler) to high.

Stir the meat mixture well, then thread the cubes on to skewers. Put the skewers on to the lined rack of the grill (broiler) pan and grill (broil) the cubes for 5 to 8 minutes on each side, or until they are cooked through.

Transfer the skewers to a warmed serving dish and sprinkle over the coriander leaves. Garnish with the lemon wedges before serving.

6 Servings

VINDALOO
(Vinegar Pork Curry)

Vindaloos come from the west coast of India and, although they are traditionally made with pork, chicken and even duck are sometimes substituted. This type of curry relies on vinegar rather than coconut milk to moisten and is rather hot.

	Metric/U.K.	U.S.
Fresh root ginger, peeled and chopped	5cm/2in piece	2in piece

A simple dish of braised, curried lambs' kidneys, Gurda Korma can be served with a selection of chutneys to make the centrepiece for a beautiful meal.

	Metric/U.K.	U.S.
Garlic cloves, chopped	4	4
Hot chilli powder	1½ tsp	1½ tsp
Turmeric	2 tsp	2 tsp
Salt	1 tsp	1 tsp
Cardamom seeds	1 Tbs	1 Tbs
Whole cloves	6	6
Peppercorns	6	6
Cinnamon stick	5cm/2in	2in
Coriander seeds	2 Tbs	2 Tbs
Cumin seeds	1 Tbs	1 Tbs
Wine vinegar	150ml/5floz	⅝ cup
Pork fillet (tenderloin), cubed	1kg/2lb	2lb
Curry leaves (optional)	4	4
Vegetable oil	3 Tbs	3 Tbs
Mustard seeds	1 tsp	1 tsp
Water	150ml/5floz	⅝ cup

Put the ginger, garlic, chilli powder, turmeric, salt, cardamom, cloves, peppercorns, cinnamon, coriander, cumin seeds and vinegar into a blender and blend to a purée. Scrape down the sides of the blender and blend for a further 30 seconds. Add more vinegar if necessary to form a smooth liquid paste.

Put the pork in a large bowl and pour over the spice paste. Cover and set aside to marinate for 1 hour. Lay the curry leaves, if you are using them, on top. Re-cover and put the bowl into the refrigerator for 24 hours, turning the meat two or three times during the period.

Two hours before cooking time, remove the bowl from refrigerator and set aside.

Heat the oil in a large saucepan. Add the mustard seeds and cover the pan. Fry the seeds until they pop, then add the pork, marinade and water and bring to the boil, stirring constantly. Reduce the heat to low, cover the pan and simmer for 30 minutes. Uncover and simmer for a further 30 minutes, or until the pork is cooked through and tender.

Transfer the vindaloo to a warmed serving dish and serve at once.

4-6 Servings

KOFTA CHASNIDARH
(Sweet and Sour Meatballs)

The Indians, too, have a sweet and sour taste although it is perhaps not so well known as the Chinese version. *This is a basic version of the technique using meatballs as the meat ingredient, but cubed beef, lamb or pork could equally be used providing the cooking time is adjusted to suit.*

	Metric/U.K.	U.S.
Minced (ground) pork	700g/1½lb	1½lb
Small onion, grated	1	1
Paprika	1 tsp	1 tsp
Ground cumin	2 tsp	2 tsp
Salt and pepper to taste		
Chick-pea flour	3 Tbs	3 Tbs
Ghee or clarified butter	50g/2oz	4 Tbs
Sugar	50g/2oz	¼ cup
Lime or lemon juice	125ml/4floz	½ cup
Cornflour (cornstarch)	1 Tbs	1 Tbs
Fresh root ginger, peeled and finely chopped	2½cm/1in piece	1in piece
Carrots, cut into lengths	2	2
Medium onions, quartered	2	2
Green pepper, pith and seeds removed and chopped	1	1
Chicken stock	300ml/10floz	1¼ cups
Saffron threads, soaked in 2 Tbs boiling water	¼ tsp	¼ tsp
Ground fenugreek	2 tsp	2 tsp

Put the pork, onion, paprika, cumin, seasoning and flour into a large bowl and mix well. Using your hands, shape the mixture into walnut-sized balls.

Melt three-quarters of the ghee or butter in a large frying-pan. Add the meatballs, a few at a time, and fry until they are deeply and evenly browned. Remove from the heat and keep hot while you make the sauce.

Mix the sugar, lime or lemon juice and cornflour (cornstarch) in a bowl until they are well blended. Set aside.

Melt the remaining ghee or butter in a saucepan. Add the ginger and fry for 1 minute, stirring constantly. Add the vegetables and fry until they are soft. Pour over the stock and bring to the boil. Stir in the sugar mixture and cook, stirring constantly, until the liquid thickens and becomes smooth. Stir in the remaining ingredients, including the reserved meatballs, and bring the liquid to the boil again. Reduce the heat to low, cover the pan and simmer for 30 to 40 minutes, or until the

	Metric/U.K.	U.S.
Small onions, chopped	2	2
Hot chilli powder	¼ tsp	¼ tsp
Ground turmeric	¼ tsp	¼ tsp
Ground coriander	1 tsp	1 tsp
Ground cumin	¼ tsp	¼ tsp
Salt and pepper to taste		
Lambs' kidneys, prepared and quartered	8	8
Small green pepper, pith and seeds removed and thinly sliced	1	1

Melt the butter with the oil in a frying-pan. Add the garlic and ginger and fry for 30 seconds. Stir in the onions and fry until they are soft. Stir in the chilli powder, turmeric, coriander and cumin and cook for 1 minute. Add the seasoning and kidneys. Stir well to coat the kidneys, then cook, stirring occasionally, for 15 minutes, or until the kidneys are only faintly pink inside.

Transfer the mixture to a warmed serving dish and arrange the green pepper on top. Serve at once.

4 Servings

Samosas are the Indian equivalent of western turnovers and are served as snacks and at picnics all over India. This particular version contains a spicy meat filling.

meatballs are cooked through and tender and the sauce has thickened.

Transfer the mixture to a warmed serving dish.

Serve at once.

4 Servings

GURDA KORMA
(Curried Kidneys)

This dish is simple in the extreme, yet the end result is both appetizing and attractive to look at (see the photograph on the previous page). Serve with plain boiled rice and a selection of chutneys and raitas.

	Metric/U.K.	U.S.
Butter	25g/1oz	2 Tbs
Vegetable oil	1 Tbs	1 Tbs
Garlic clove, crushed	1	1
Fresh root ginger, peeled and finely chopped	1cm/½in piece	½in piece

NARGISI KOFTAS
(Meatballs Stuffed with Hard-Boiled Eggs)

This dish is the Indian equivalent of the western Scotch eggs and, like Scotch eggs, is usually served as a snack or picnic dish. They can, however, be served with a tomato or curry sauce over rice.

	Metric/U.K.	U.S.
Minced (ground) lamb	575g/1¼lb	1¼lb
Fresh root ginger, peeled and finely chopped	2½cm/1in piece	1in piece
Hot chilli powder	½ tsp	½ tsp
Ground cumin	1 tsp	1 tsp
Ground coriander	1 Tbs	1 Tbs
Onion, finely chopped	1	1
Garlic cloves, crushed	2	2
Chick-pea flour	40g/1½oz	⅓ cup
Salt and pepper to taste		
Egg	1	1
Hard-boiled eggs	8	8

Sufficient vegetable oil
for deep-frying

Combine the lamb, ginger, chilli powder, cumin, coriander, onion, garlic, flour, seasoning and egg. Using your hands, mix and knead well until the ingredients are thoroughly blended. Alternatively, purée the ginger, onion and garlic together in a blender before adding them to the other ingredients.

Divide the mixture into eight equal portions. Using wet hands, roll each portion into a ball, then flatten and put a hard-boiled egg in the centre. Bring the meat mixture up and around the egg to enclose it completely. Put the balls into a greased dish and chill in the refrigerator for 30 minutes.

Fill a deep-frying pan one-third full with oil and heat until it reaches 190°C (375°F) on a deep-fat thermometer, or until a small cube of stale bread dropped into the oil turns golden in 40 seconds. Carefully lower the balls into the oil, a few at a time, and fry for 2 to 3 minutes or until they are golden brown and crisp. Remove the koftas from the oil and drain on kitchen towels.

Arrange on a warmed serving dish and serve at once.

4-6 Servings

SAMOSAS
(Stuffed Savoury Pastries)

These spicy little pastries are served both as picnic or other snacks, or as part of a meal in India. This version contains meat, but a selection of finely chopped vegetables can be substituted if you prefer.

	Metric/U.K.	U.S.
PASTRY		
Flour	225g/8oz	2 cups
Salt	½ tsp	½ tsp
Butter	25g/1oz	2 Tbs
Water	50-75ml/ 2-3floz	¼ to ⅜ cup
FILLING		
Butter	25g/1oz	2 Tbs
Small onion, finely chopped	1	1
Garlic cloves, crushed	2	2
Green chillis, chopped	2	2
Fresh root ginger, peeled and finely chopped	2½cm/1in piece	1in piece
Turmeric	½ tsp	½ tsp
Hot chilli powder	½ tsp	½ tsp
Lean minced (ground) beef	350g/12oz	12oz
Salt	1 tsp	1 tsp
Garam masala	2 tsp	2 tsp
Juice of ½ lemon		
Sufficient vegetable oil for deep-frying		

First make the pastry. Sift the flour and salt into a bowl. Add the butter, cut into small pieces, and rub it into the flour until the mixture resembles fine breadcrumbs. Pour in 50ml/ 2floz (¼ cup) of water and mix with a knife to a smooth dough. Add a little more water if the dough looks too dry. Pat the dough into a ball and turn it out on to a lightly floured surface. Knead it well for 10 minutes, or until the dough is smooth and elastic. Return the dough to the bowl, cover and set aside while you make the filling.

Melt the butter in a frying-pan. Add the onion, garlic, chillis and ginger and fry until the onion is golden brown. Stir in the turmeric and chilli powder, then the meat and salt. Cook, stirring constantly, until the meat is cooked through and all the moisture has been absorbed. Stir in the garam masala and lemon juice and cook for a further 5 minutes. Remove the pan from the heat and set aside to cool.

Divide the dough into 15 equal portions. Roll each portion into a ball. Flatten each ball and roll out to a circle about 10cm/4in in diameter. Cut each circle in half. Dampen the cut edges of each semi-circle with water and shape them into cones. Fill the cones with a little of the filling, dampen the top and bottom edges of the cones and pinch together to seal. Set aside.

Fill a deep-frying pan one third full with oil and heat until it reaches 185°C (360°F) on a deep-fat thermometer, or until a small cube of stale bread dropped into the oil turns golden in 50 seconds.

Carefully lower the samosas into the oil, a few at a time, and fry them for 2 to 3 minutes, or until they are golden brown. Remove from the oil and drain on kitchen towels.

Pile on to a warmed serving dish and serve at once.

30 Samosas

Poultry and Game

Masalas in Indian cooking are spice mixtures, which form the basis of many dishes. Usually the ingredients for a masala are balanced finely so that although each one can be tasted separately, no one dominates the mixture. However, occasionally one spice is deliberately allowed to predominate. In this superb chicken dish, Zeera Murg, the principal spice is cumin, and the result is absolutely fantastic!

TANDOORI MURG
(Marinated Spiced Chicken)

Tandoori in Indian cooking indicates that the main ingredient (usually lamb or chicken) has been cooked in a special clay oven called a tandoor. You can, however, use a domestic oven instead—in this case, either put the chicken on a rack in a roasting pan or on a spit. Traditionally tandoori chicken is served with sliced onions, tomatoes and green chillis.

	Metric/U.K.	U.S.
Chicken, skinned	1x1½kg/3lb	1x3lb
Hot chilli powder	1 tsp	1 tsp
Salt and pepper to taste		
Lemon juice	2 Tbs	2 Tbs
Butter, melted	50g/2oz	4 Tbs
MARINADE		
Yogurt	3 Tbs	3 Tbs
Garlic cloves	4	4
Raisins	1 Tbs	1 Tbs
Fresh root ginger, peeled and finely chopped	5cm/2in piece	2in piece
Cumin seeds	1 tsp	1 tsp
Coriander seeds	1 Tbs	1 Tbs
Dried red chillis	2	2
Orange or red food colouring	½ tsp	½ tsp

Make gashes in the thighs and on each side of the breast of the chicken. Mix the chilli powder, seasoning to taste and lemon juice together, then rub the mixture all over the bird, especially into the gashes. Set aside for 20 minutes.

Meanwhile, prepare the marinade. Put all the ingredients, except the red food colouring, into a blender and purée until smooth. Transfer the mixture to a small bowl and stir in the food colouring. Put the chicken in a large bowl and spread the yogurt mixture all over the chicken, rubbing it well into the gashes. Cover the bowl and chill in the refrigerator for 24 hours.

Preheat the oven to fairly hot 200°C (Gas Mark 6, 400°F).

Put the chicken, on its back, on a rack in a roasting pan. Pour in enough water just to cover the bottom of the pan—this is to prevent the drippings from burning. Spoon all the marinade left in the bowl over the chicken, then a tablespoon of the melted butter. Roast the chicken for 1 hour, or until it is very tender, basting frequently with the remaining melted butter and the drippings in the pan.

Remove the pan from the oven. Put the chicken on a carving board and cut into serving pieces. Arrange the pieces on a warmed platter. Scrape any drippings from the pan and spoon over the chicken. Serve at once.

2-3 Servings

ZEERA MURG
(Cumin Chicken)

	Metric/U.K.	U.S.
Chicken, cut into 8 serving pieces	1x2½kg/5lb	1x5lb
Juice of 2 lemons		
Salt	1 tsp	1 tsp
Cayenne pepper	1 tsp	1 tsp
Flour	25g/1oz	¼ cup
Butter	50g/2oz	4 Tbs
Onions, sliced	2	2
Garlic cloves, crushed	2	2
Fresh root ginger, peeled and finely chopped	2½cm/1in piece	1in piece
Cumin seeds	2 tsp	2 tsp
Yogurt	300ml/10floz	1¼ cups
Double (heavy) cream	150ml/5floz	⅝ cup
Thinly pared rind of 1 lemon, in one piece		

Put the chicken pieces on a large plate and rub them all over with the lemon juice. Set aside for 20 minutes, then pat dry with kitchen towels.

Mix the salt, cayenne and flour together on a second plate and roll the chicken pieces in it, shaking off any excess.

Melt the butter in a frying-pan. Add the chicken pieces and fry until they are evenly

browned. As they brown, transfer the pieces to a plate.

Add the onions, garlic, ginger and cumin seeds to the pan and fry until they are golden brown. Stir in the yogurt, cream and lemon rind. Return the chicken pieces to the pan and turn in the mixture to coat thoroughly. Bring to the boil, reduce the heat to low and cover. Simmer the chicken for 1 hour, or until it is cooked through and tender. Uncover the pan for the last 20 minutes to allow the sauce to thicken somewhat.

Chicken Tikka is a popular Pakistani dish in which small cubes of chicken meat are marinated overnight in yogurt, then grilled (broiled).

Discard the lemon rind and transfer the chicken and sauce to a warmed serving dish. Serve at once.

6 Servings

CHICKEN TIKKA
(Spicy Chicken Kebabs)

This is one of the most popular Pakistani dishes, and is usually accompanied by naan or chappati.

	Metric/U.K.	U.S.
Yogurt	150ml/5floz	$\frac{5}{8}$ cup
Garlic cloves, crushed	4	4
Fresh root ginger, peeled and finely chopped	4cm/1½in piece	1½in piece
Small onion, grated	1	1
Hot chilli powder	1½ tsp	1½ tsp
Ground coriander	1 Tbs	1 Tbs

	Metric/U.K.	U.S.
Salt	1 tsp	1 tsp
Chicken breasts, skinned and boned	4	4
GARNISH		
Large onion, thinly sliced into rings	1	1
Large tomatoes, thinly sliced	2	2
Chopped coriander leaves	2 Tbs	2 Tbs

Combine the yogurt, garlic, ginger, onion, chilli powder, coriander and salt together. Set aside.

Cut the chicken meat into 2½cm/1in cubes. Add the cubes to the marinade and mix well. Cover the bowl and chill in the refrigerator for at least 6 hours, or overnight.

Preheat the grill (broiler) to high.

Thread the chicken cubes on to skewers. Place the skewers on a lined rack in the grill (broiler) pan and grill (broil) the cubes, turning them occasionally, for 5 to 8 minutes, or until they are cooked through.

Remove the skewers from the heat and slide the kebabs on to a warmed serving dish. Garnish with the onion rings, tomatoes and coriander leaves and serve at once.

4 Servings

GOAN VINEGAR CURRY

The Goan Christians are a minority religious group who live in the former Portuguese colony of Goa on the west coast of India. Their cooking, like that of the Syrian Christians, is distinctively different from that of their Indian neighbours, and includes (unusual in India) a great many pork dishes. This particular curry uses chicken but pork could be substituted if you prefer.

	Metric/U.K.	U.S.
Vegetable oil	75ml/3floz	⅜ cup
Fresh root ginger, peeled and finely chopped	7½cm/3in piece	3in piece
Green chillis, chopped	3	3
Garlic cloves, chopped	4	4
Chicken, cut into 8 serving pieces	1x2kg/4lb	1x4lb
Ground cardamom	½ tsp	½ tsp
Ground cloves	½ tsp	½ tsp
Ground cinnamon	½ tsp	½ tsp
Turmeric	1½ tsp	1½ tsp
Ground coriander	1 Tbs	1 Tbs
Hot chilli powder	½ tsp	½ tsp
Vinegar	250ml/8floz	1 cup
Large onions, sliced	4	4
Water	150ml/5floz	⅝ cup
Salt	1 tsp	1 tsp

Heat the oil in a large saucepan. Add the ginger, chillis and garlic and fry for 2 minutes, stirring constantly. Add the chicken pieces and fry until they are evenly browned. Transfer the chicken pieces to a plate and set aside.

Mix the cardamom, cloves, cinnamon, turmeric, coriander and chilli powder with enough of the vinegar to make a paste.

Add the onions to the pan and fry until they are golden brown. Stir in the spice paste and fry for 8 minutes, stirring constantly. Add a spoonful or two of vinegar if the mixture becomes too dry.

Return the chicken pieces to the pan and pour in the remaining vinegar, the water and salt. Bring to the boil, cover the pan and reduce the heat to low. Simmer for 1 hour, or until the chicken is cooked through and tender.

Transfer to a warmed serving dish and serve at once.

4-6 Servings

MURGHI BIRYANI
(Chicken with Rice)

The only real difference between biryanis and pulaos is that in the former the rice is partially and the meat completely cooked before being baked together.

	Metric/U.K.	U.S.
Ghee or clarified butter	125g/4oz	8 Tbs
Garlic cloves, crushed	3	3
Fresh root ginger, peeled and finely chopped	4cm/1½in piece	1½in piece
Cayenne pepper	½ tsp	½ tsp
Cumin seeds	1½ tsp	1½ tsp
Chicken cut into serving pieces	1x2½kg/5lb	1x5lb

Cinnamon stick	1x10cm/4in	1x4in
Cloves	10	10
Peppercorns	8	8
Cardamom seeds	1 tsp	1 tsp
Yogurt	350ml/12floz	1½ cups
Salt	2 tsp	2 tsp
Long-grain rice, soaked in cold water for 30 minutes and drained	450g/1lb	2⅔ cups
Saffron threads, soaked in 2 Tbs boiling water	1 tsp	1 tsp
Onions, thinly sliced	2	2
Slivered almonds	75g/3oz	½ cup
Sultanas or seedless raisins	50g/2oz	⅓ cup

Melt half the ghee or clarified butter in a large saucepan. Add the garlic, ginger, cayenne and cumin seeds and fry for 3 minutes. Add the chicken pieces and fry until they are evenly browned. Stir in the cinnamon, cloves, peppercorns, cardamom, yogurt, and half the salt. Add 125ml/4floz (½ cup) of water and bring to the boil. Reduce the heat to low, cover the pan and simmer for 1 hour, or until the chicken is cooked through and tender.

Bring 1½l/3 pints (4 pints) water to the boil in a large saucepan. Add the remaining salt and pour in the rice. Boil briskly for 1½ minutes. Remove from the heat, drain the rice and set aside.

Preheat the oven to moderate 180°C (Gas Mark 4, 350°F).

Melt 1 tablespoon of the remaining ghee in a large flameproof casserole. Put one-third of the parboiled rice over the bottom, then cover with one-third of the chicken. Sprinkle one-third of the saffron mixture over it. Cover with another one-third of the chicken pieces, then with rice, sprinkled with saffron water. Remove all the remaining chicken pieces from the pan and arrange them on top. Finish with a final layer of rice, sprinkled with saffron water. Pour over the pan liquid. Cover the casserole tightly and put into the oven. Cook for 20 to 30 minutes, or until the rice is tender and the liquid is absorbed.

Melt the remaining ghee or clarified butter in a small frying-pan. Add the onions and fry until they are golden brown. Using a slotted spoon, transfer to a plate. Add the almonds and sultanas or seedless raisins to the pan and fry for 3 minutes, or until the almonds are toasted. Using the slotted spoon, transfer the nuts and

raisins to the onions.

Transfer the rice and chicken to a large warmed serving dish and sprinkle over the onions, almonds and raisins. Serve at once.

6-8 Servings

RUSTOM'S CHICKEN

	Metric/U.K.	U.S.
Garlic cloves, crushed	2	2
Salt	1½ tsp	1½ tsp
Lemon juice	2 Tbs	2 Tbs
Chicken, cut into serving pieces	1x2kg/4lb	1x4lb
Vegetable oil	50ml/2floz	¼ cup
Medium onions, sliced	3	3
Green chillis, chopped	2	2
Fresh root ginger, peeled and finely chopped	2½cm/1in piece	1in piece
Turmeric	1 tsp	1 tsp
Ground almonds	2 Tbs	2 Tbs
Chicken stock	250ml/8floz	1 cup
RICE Butter	25g/1oz	2 Tbs
Medium onion, chopped	1	1
Sugar	1½ tsp	1½ tsp
Water	125ml/4floz	½ cup
Long-grain rice, soaked in cold water for 30 minutes and drained	350g/12oz	2 cups
Cardamom seeds	1 Tbs	1 Tbs
Salt	1 tsp	1 tsp
GARNISH Butter	25g/1oz	2 Tbs
Large bananas, peeled, sliced in half lengthways, then halved	2	2
Chopped unsalted cashew nuts, roasted	3 Tbs	3 Tbs
Chopped coriander leaves	1 Tbs	1 Tbs

Combine the garlic, salt and lemon juice together and rub all over the chicken pieces. Set aside for 1 hour.

Heat the oil in a large frying-pan. Add the onions and fry until they are golden brown.

Rustom's Chicken is an exotic mixture of chicken with ground almonds, served with a garnish of roasted cashew nuts and bananas.

Dhansak is a classic Parsee dish from the west coast of India, a mixture of chicken, lentils and vegetables.

Stir in the chillis, ginger and turmeric and fry for 1 minute. Add the chicken pieces and fry until they are evenly browned. Stir in the ground almonds and fry for 1 minute. Pour in the stock and stir to mix. Reduce the heat to low, cover the pan and simmer for 50 minutes, or until the chicken is cooked through.

Meanwhile, cook the rice. Melt the butter in a saucepan. Add the onion and fry until it is soft. Stir in the sugar and cook until it is brown and caramelized. Stir in the water and bring to the boil, stirring constantly. Add the rice, cardamom seeds and salt and stir to mix. Add just enough water to cover the rice by about 1cm/½in. Bring to the boil, reduce the heat to low and cover the pan. Simmer the rice for 15 to 20 minutes, or until it is tender.

While the rice is cooking, prepare the garnish. Melt the butter in a small frying-pan. Add the banana slices and fry for 3 minutes, or until they are golden.

Spoon the rice on to a serving dish. Arrange the chicken pieces on top and pour over the cooking juices from the pan. Scatter the cashew nuts over the top and sprinkle over the coriander leaves. Arrange the banana slices around the chicken and serve at once.

4-6 Servings

DHANSAK
(Chicken with Lentils and Vegetables)

The Parsees are an important religious sect whose members fled from Persia hundreds of years ago and settled mainly on the west coast of India. They have remained intact as a community and their cooking is quite distinctive. This is one of their most famous dishes, and although it is normally made with chicken, as here, lamb can be substituted. The dhals mentioned here are merely different forms of lentils; if you cannot obtain them all, the more common red or yellow lentils may be substituted.

	Metric/U.K.	U.S.
Tur dhal (lentils)	125g/4oz	½ cup
Channa dhal (lentils)	25g/1oz	⅛ cup
Masoor dhal (lentils)	50g/2oz	¼ cup
Moong dhal (lentils)	25g/1oz	⅛ cup
Water	900ml/1½ pints	3¾ cups
Salt	2 tsp	2 tsp
Ghee or clarified butter	40g/1½oz	3 Tbs
Fresh root ginger, peeled and finely chopped	2½cm/1in piece	1in piece

	Metric/U.K.	U.S.
Garlic clove, finely chopped	1	1
Chicken pieces	8	8
Chopped fresh mint	1 Tbs	1 Tbs
Aubergine (eggplant), cubed	1	1
Pumpkin, peeled and cubed	225g/8oz	$1\frac{1}{3}$ cups
Spinach, chopped	125g/4oz	1 cup
Large onion, sliced	1	1
Canned peeled tomatoes, drained	425g/14oz	14oz
MASALA		
Ghee or clarified butter	50g/2oz	4 Tbs
Large onion, sliced	1	1
Fresh root ginger, peeled and sliced	4cm/$1\frac{1}{2}$in piece	$1\frac{1}{2}$in piece
Green chillis, finely chopped	2	2
Garlic cloves, crushed	3	3
Ground cinnamon	$\frac{1}{2}$ tsp	$\frac{1}{2}$ tsp
Ground cardamom	$\frac{1}{2}$ tsp	$\frac{1}{2}$ tsp
Ground cloves	$\frac{1}{2}$ tsp	$\frac{1}{2}$ tsp
Turmeric	$1\frac{1}{2}$ tsp	$1\frac{1}{2}$ tsp
Ground coriander	1 tsp	1 tsp
Hot chilli powder	$\frac{1}{2}$ tsp	$\frac{1}{2}$ tsp
Chopped coriander leaves	3 Tbs	3 Tbs

Wash all the dhals thoroughly and soak them for 30 minutes in cold water. Drain and transfer them to a large saucepan. Add the water and salt and bring to the boil, skimming off any scum. Reduce the heat to low, cover the pan and simmer for 40 minutes.

Meanwhile, heat the ghee or clarified butter in a large frying-pan. Add the ginger and garlic and fry for 2 minutes, stirring constantly. Add the chicken pieces and fry until they are deeply and evenly browned. Transfer the mixture to the dhal.

Add the mint, aubergine (eggplant), pumpkin, spinach, onion and tomatoes. Increase the heat to high, stir to mix and bring to the boil. Reduce the heat to low, cover the pan and simmer for 45 minutes, or until the chicken is cooked through and tender. Transfer the chicken pieces to a plate. Purée the vegetables and dhal in a blender and set aside.

Rinse out and dry the saucepan. To make the masala, heat the ghee or clarified butter in the saucepan. Add the onion and fry until golden brown. Stir in the ginger, chillis and garlic and fry for 3 minutes. Stir in all the remaining ingredients, except the coriander leaves, and fry for 8 minutes, stirring constantly. Add a spoonful or two of water if the mixture becomes too dry. Pour the puréed vegetables and dhal mixture into the pan and stir well. Bring to the boil, reduce the heat to low and cover the pan. Simmer the mixture for 20 minutes. Stir in the chicken pieces and simmer for a further 10 minutes, basting the chicken with the sauce.

Transfer the dhansak to a warmed serving dish, sprinkle over the coriander leaves and serve at once.

6-8 Servings

MURG KASHMIRI
(Chicken with Almonds and Raisins)

	Metric/U.K.	U.S.
Chicken, skinned	1x2kg/4lb	1x4lb
Juice of $\frac{1}{2}$ lemon		
Coriander seeds	1 Tbs	1 Tbs
Black peppercorns	1 tsp	1 tsp
Cardamom seeds	1 tsp	1 tsp
Whole cloves	6	6
Fresh root ginger, peeled and finely chopped	4cm/$1\frac{1}{2}$in piece	$1\frac{1}{2}$in piece
Salt	1 tsp	1 tsp
Hot chilli powder	$\frac{1}{2}$ tsp	$\frac{1}{2}$ tsp
Butter	75g/3oz	6 Tbs
Medium onions, very finely chopped	2	2
Double (heavy) cream	300ml/10floz	$1\frac{1}{4}$ cups
Saffron threads, soaked in 2 Tbs boiling water	$\frac{1}{4}$ tsp	$\frac{1}{4}$ tsp
Slivered almonds	50g/2oz	$\frac{1}{3}$ cup
Raisins	50g/2oz	$\frac{1}{3}$ cup

Preheat the oven to fairly hot 200°C (Gas Mark 6, 400°F). Prick the chicken all over, then rub over the lemon juice. Set aside.

Using a mortar and pestle, or grinder, crush the coriander seeds, peppercorns, cardamom seeds and cloves. Sift the spices through a fine strainer into a small bowl. Stir in the ginger, salt and chilli powder. Using a small wooden spoon, cream in half the butter to make a smooth paste. Rub the paste all over the chicken, then transfer the chicken to a flameproof casserole. Put the casserole into the oven and roast the chicken for 15 minutes.

Meanwhile, melt the remaining butter in a saucepan. Add the onions and fry until they are golden brown. Remove from the heat and stir in the cream, saffron mixture, almonds and raisins. Pour over the chicken.

Reduce the oven temperature to moderate 180°C (Gas Mark 4, 350°F) and roast the chicken, basting every 10 minutes with the cream and almond mixture, for a further 1 hour, or until it is cooked through and tender.

Remove from the oven and transfer the chicken to a carving board. Carve into serving pieces and arrange them on a warmed serving dish. Keep hot while you finish the sauce.

Skim off most of the fat from the surface of the cooking liquid. Return to low heat and simmer the sauce for 2 minutes, stirring constantly. Pour over the chicken pieces and serve at once.

4 Servings

MURG MASSALAM
(Baked Spiced Chicken)

This is one of the great Moghul dishes of northern India, rich yet rather delicate. Although traditionally the chicken is baked whole, if you prefer, it can be cut into serving pieces.

	Metric/U.K.	U.S.
Chicken	1x2kg/4lb	1x4lb
Juice of 1½ lemons		
Salt	2 tsp	2 tsp
Cayenne pepper	1 tsp	1 tsp
Saffron threads, soaked in 2 Tbs boiling water	¼ tsp	¼ tsp
Butter, melted	50g/2oz	4 Tbs
MARINADE		
Raisins	50g/2oz	⅓ cup
Flaked almonds	75g/3oz	½ cup
Clear honey	1 Tbs	1 Tbs
Garlic cloves	2	2
Fresh root ginger, peeled and finely chopped	5cm/2in piece	2in piece
Cardamom seeds	½ tsp	½ tsp
Cumin seeds	½ tsp	½ tsp
Turmeric	1 tsp	1 tsp
Yogurt	150ml/5floz	⅝ cup
Double (heavy) cream	125ml/4floz	½ cup

Make diagonal cuts in the breast and thighs of the chicken. Combine the lemon juice, salt and cayenne, then rub the mixture all over the chicken, pushing it well into the slits. Put the chicken into a bowl and set aside for 30 minutes.

Meanwhile, make the marinade. Put the raisins, almonds, honey, garlic, ginger, cardamom, cumin and turmeric into a blender. Add 4 tablespoons of yogurt and purée to a smooth paste, adding more yogurt if necessary. Transfer the purée to a bowl and stir in the remaining yogurt and cream.

Pour the marinade over the chicken, cover the bowl and marinate in the refrigerator for 24 hours, turning the chicken over occasionally. Remove from the refrigerator and set aside at room temperature for 1 hour.

Preheat the oven to fairly hot 200°C (Gas Mark 6, 400°F).

Put the chicken into a deep roasting pan. Combine the saffron mixture with the remaining marinade in the bowl and pour over the chicken. Spoon a little of the melted butter over the top. Pour 150ml/5floz (⅝ cup) of water into the pan and put the pan into the oven. Roast the chicken, basting frequently with the liquid in the pan, for 1 hour, or until the chicken is cooked through and tender.

Remove the pan from the oven and transfer the chicken to a warmed serving dish. Spoon the cooking juices over the chicken and serve at once.

4 Servings

PAKISTANI PULAO
(Curried Chicken with Rice)

	Metric/U.K.	U.S.
Ghee or clarified butter	50g/2oz	4 Tbs
Large onion, sliced	1	1
Fresh root ginger, peeled and finely chopped	4cm/1½in piece	1½in piece
Garlic cloves, crushed	2	2
Green chillis, chopped	2	2
Chicken, cut into		

serving pieces	1x2kg/4lb	1x4lb
Turmeric	1 tsp	1 tsp
Hot chilli powder	½ tsp	½ tsp
Ground coriander	1 Tbs	1 Tbs
Salt	1½ tsp	1½ tsp
Black pepper	½ tsp	½ tsp
Yogurt	150ml/5floz	⅝ cup

Juice of 1 small lemon		
Long-grain rice, soaked in cold water for 30 minutes and drained	350g/12oz	2 cups
Boiling water	350ml/12floz	1½ cups

Melt the ghee or butter in a large saucepan. Add the onion and fry until it is soft. Add the ginger, garlic and chillis, reduce the heat to low

Murg Massalam, below left, is one of the great Moghul chicken dishes of northern India ; below right is a delicate, unusual dish of Curried Partridges.

An unusual and pungent curry, Duck Curry is cooked in a vinegar-based masala and coconut milk.

and fry for 4 minutes, stirring occasionally. Add the chicken pieces and fry them until they are evenly browned.

Combine the remaining spices, salt, pepper, yogurt and lemon juice in a bowl. Pour the mixture into the pan and mix well. Reduce the heat to low, cover and simmer for 35 to 40 minutes, or until the chicken is almost cooked.

Uncover the pan and increase the heat to moderately high. Stir in the rice and cook, stirring frequently, until most of the liquid in the pan has been absorbed. Pour in the water and cover the pan. When the water begins to boil again, reduce the heat to low and simmer for 15 to 20 minutes, or until the rice is tender

and all the liquid has been absorbed.

Remove from the heat and serve at once.

4-6 Servings

CURRIED PARTRIDGES

	Metric/U.K.	U.S.
Juice of 1 lemon		
Salt	1½ tsp	1½ tsp
Partridges, oven-ready and with the giblets		

reserved	4	4
Water	900ml/1½ pints	3¾ cups
Whole cloves	4	4
Fresh root ginger, peeled and finely chopped	2½cm/1in piece	1in piece
Garlic cloves, chopped	4	4
Onion, halved	1	1
Butter	50g/2oz	4 Tbs
Medium onions, finely chopped	2	2
Ground coriander	2 tsp	2 tsp
Cayenne pepper	1 tsp	1 tsp
Single (light) cream	300ml/10floz	1¼ cups
Ground almonds	125g/4oz	⅔ cup
Cardamom seeds, crushed	1 tsp	1 tsp
Saffron threads, soaked in 2 Tbs boiling water	¼ tsp	¼ tsp

Mix the lemon juice with 1 teaspoon of salt, then rub the mixture all over the partridges. Set aside while you make the stock.

Bring the giblets, water, cloves, ginger, garlic and halved onion to the boil in a saucepan. Reduce the heat to low, cover the pan and simmer for 1½ hours. Remove from the heat and strain into a bowl. Rinse and dry the pan. Return the stock to the pan and bring to the boil again. Boil until it reduces to about 300ml/10floz (1¼ cups).

Melt the butter in a flameproof casserole. Add the chopped onions and fry until they are golden brown. Stir in the coriander and cayenne and cook for 3 minutes, stirring constantly. Add the partridges and fry until they are deeply and evenly browned.

Pour over the reserved stock and season with the remaining salt. Bring to the boil, reduce the heat to low and cover the pan. Simmer for 20 minutes. Uncover, increase the heat to moderately low and simmer for a further 25 minutes, or until the partridges are cooked through and tender and the liquid has evaporated.

Preheat the oven to cool 150°C (Gas Mark 2, 300°F).

Combine the cream, almonds, cardamom and the saffron mixture. Pour the mixture over the partridges and stir to mix. Bring to the boil, cover the casserole and put into the oven. Cook for 20 minutes, then serve at once.

4 Servings

DUCK CURRY

This basic curry combines the rich taste of duck with a vinegar-based masala and coconut milk— and the result is absolutely superb!

	Metric/U.K.	U.S.
Ghee or clarified butter	75g/3oz	6 Tbs
Duck, cut into serving pieces	1x3kg/6lb	1x6lb
Mustard seeds	1 tsp	1 tsp
Medium onions, finely chopped	3	3
Garlic cloves, finely chopped	2	2
Fresh root ginger, peeled and finely chopped	4cm/1½in piece	1½in piece
Green chilli, finely chopped	1	1
Ground cumin	1 tsp	1 tsp
Hot chilli powder	1 tsp	1 tsp
Ground coriander	1 Tbs	1 Tbs
Garam masala	1 Tbs	1 Tbs
Turmeric	1 tsp	1 tsp
Salt	½ tsp	½ tsp
Vinegar	3 Tbs	3 Tbs
Coconut milk	350ml/12floz	1½ cups

Melt the ghee or clarified butter in a large saucepan. Add the duck pieces and fry until they are evenly browned. Transfer them to a plate.

Add the mustard seeds to the pan, cover and fry them until they begin to pop. Add the onions and fry until they are golden brown. Add the garlic, ginger and chilli and fry for 3 minutes, stirring frequently.

Put the cumin, chilli powder, coriander, garam masala, turmeric and salt into a bowl and stir in the vinegar to make a smooth paste. Add the paste to the saucepan and fry for 8 minutes, stirring constantly. Return the duck pieces to the pan and baste well with the paste. Fry for 3 minutes. Pour over the coconut milk and stir well to mix. Reduce the heat to low, cover the pan and simmer for 1 hour, or until the duck pieces are cooked through and tender, and the gravy is thick.

Transfer the mixture to a warmed serving dish and serve at once.

4 Servings

Fish and Seafood

Two fabulous deep-fried dishes: above Talawa Gosht, deep-fried lean lamb cubes and potatoes (recipe page 24); below Tali Machee, deep-fried spiced sole fillets.

BANGRA MASALA
(Spiced Herrings)

This dish is from the west coast of India, where fish is abundant and plays an important part in the staple diet. Bangra is a fish found around the coasts; it looks and tastes somewhat like herrings, which is why we have suggested them as a substitute here.

	Metric/U.K.	U.S.
Herrings, cleaned and gutted	4	4
Salt	2½ tsp	2½ tsp
Juice of ½ lemon		
Flour	3 Tbs	3 Tbs
Turmeric	1 tsp	1 tsp
Vegetable oil	50ml/2floz	¼ cup
STUFFING Vegetable oil	3 Tbs	3 Tbs
Small onions, finely minced (ground)	2	2
Large garlic clove, crushed	1	1
Fresh root ginger, peeled and finely chopped	4cm/1½in piece	1½in piece
Turmeric	1 tsp	1 tsp
Ground coriander	1 tsp	1 tsp
Hot chilli powder	½ tsp	½ tsp
Garam masala	1 tsp	1 tsp
Tomato purée (paste)	75g/3oz	⅜ cup
Juice of ½ lemon		

Sprinkle the insides of the herrings with the salt and set aside.

To make the stuffing, heat the oil in a frying-pan. Add the onions and fry until they are golden brown. Add the garlic and ginger and fry for 2 minutes, stirring constantly. Stir in the turmeric, coriander, chilli powder and garam masala and fry for 8 minutes, stirring constantly. Add a spoonful or two of water if the mixture becomes too dry. Add the tomato purée (paste) and lemon juice and cook for 3 minutes. Divide the stuffing into four portions and stuff into the fish. Secure with a trussing needle and thread.

Make slits along the sides of the herrings and rub in a little lemon juice. Mix the flour, turmeric and a little salt on a plate and coat the fish in the mixture, shaking off any excess.

Heat the oil in a large frying-pan. Add the fish and fry for 10 to 15 minutes, or until they are crisp and the flesh flakes easily.

Transfer to a warmed serving dish and serve at once.

4 Servings

TALI MACHEE
(Deep-Fried Spiced Fish)

	Metric/U.K.	U.S.
Lemon sole fillets	8	8
Salt and pepper to taste		
Juice of 2 lemons		
Sufficient vegetable oil for deep-frying		
BATTER Chick-pea flour	75g/3oz	¾ cup
Rice flour	25g/1oz	¼ cup
Turmeric	1 tsp	1 tsp
Hot chilli powder	1 tsp	1 tsp
Cold water	125ml/4floz	½ cup

Cut each fillet in half, then rub all over with salt and pepper. Put the fish pieces in a large bowl and sprinkle over the lemon juice. Set aside to marinate for 1 hour.

Meanwhile, to make the batter, sift the flour, rice flour, turmeric and chilli powder into a bowl. Stir in the water until the mixture forms a smooth batter.

Remove the fish from the marinade and pat dry with kitchen towels. Dip each fish piece in the batter and set aside.

Fill a deep-frying pan one-third full with vegetable oil and heat until it reaches 180°C (350°F) on a deep-fat thermometer, or until a small cube of stale bread dropped into the oil turns golden in 55 seconds. Carefully lower the fish pieces into the oil, a few at a time, and fry for 5 minutes, or until they are crisp and golden brown. Remove from the oil and drain on kitchen towels.

Transfer to a warmed serving dish and serve at once.

4 Servings

TANDOORI MACHEE
(Marinated Spiced Fish)

The traditional items cooked in a tandoor, or clay oven, include breads and chicken; fish is a late addition and is usually only cooked in this manner in India around the west coast, where the fish and seafood are plentiful.

	Metric/U.K.	U.S.
Large red mullets, or any oily fish, cleaned and gutted	4	4
Juice of 2 lemons		
Butter, melted	75g/3oz	6 Tbs
Ground cumin	2 tsp	2 tsp
Lemon, thinly sliced	1	1
MARINADE Yogurt	50ml/2floz	$\frac{1}{4}$ cup
Garlic cloves, crushed	2	2
Fresh root ginger, peeled and finely chopped	4cm/1½in piece	1½in piece
Coriander seeds	1 Tbs	1 Tbs
Garam masala	1 tsp	1 tsp
Dried red chillis	2	2
Red food colouring	$\frac{1}{4}$ tsp	$\frac{1}{4}$ tsp

Make slits along both sides of the fish, about 2½cm/1in apart. Rub all over with the lemon juice and set aside for 10 minutes.

To make the marinade, put all the ingredients, except the food colouring, into a blender and purée until smooth. Stir in the food colouring. Put the fish into a large bowl and spoon over the marinade, turning the fish in it to coat thoroughly. Set aside to marinate at room temperature for 6 hours, basting occasionally.

Preheat the oven to fairly hot 190°C (Gas Mark 5, 375°F).

Remove the fish from the marinade and arrange them on individual skewers. Put into a rack in a deep roasting pan and put the pan into the oven. Roast the fish for 10 minutes. Combine the melted butter and ground cumin together, then brush over the fish. Return the

fish to the oven and roast for a further 5 to 8 minutes, or until the flesh flakes easily.

Remove from the oven and slide the fish on to a warmed serving dish. Garnish with the lemon slices and serve at once.

4 Servings

TAMATAR MACHEE
(Tomato Fish)

	Metric/U.K.	U.S.
Turmeric	2 tsp	2 tsp
Salt	1 tsp	1 tsp
Firm white fish fillets, skinned, boned and cubed	1kg/2lb	2lb
Vegetable oil	50ml/2floz	¼ cup
Medium onions, sliced	2	2
Hot chilli powder	1 tsp	1 tsp
Sugar	1 tsp	1 tsp
Garam masala	2 tsp	2 tsp
Ground coriander	1 Tbs	1 Tbs
Tomatoes, blanched, peeled, seeded and chopped	½kg/1lb	1lb
Sour cream	2 Tbs	2 Tbs
Lemon juice	1 Tbs	1 Tbs
Green chillis, slit in half lengthways and seeded	4	4

Mix 1½ teaspoons of turmeric and the salt on a plate. Rub the mixture over the fish cubes and set aside.

Heat the oil in a deep frying-pan. Add the fish cubes and fry until they are evenly browned. Transfer the cubes to a plate.

Jhinga Kari I, a delicious prawn (shrimp) curry from the west coast of India.

Add the onions to the pan and fry until they are golden brown. Stir in the chilli powder, sugar, garam masala, coriander and remaining turmeric. Cook for 2 minutes, stirring constantly. Stir in the tomatoes, sour cream, lemon juice and chillis and bring to the boil. Reduce the heat to low and simmer for 15 minutes.

Return the fish cubes to the pan and baste well to coat them with the sauce. Simmer for a further 10 minutes, or until the fish flakes easily.

Transfer the mixture to a warmed serving dish and serve at once.

6 Servings

WHITE FISH CURRY

	Metric/U.K.	U.S.
Vegetable oil	3 Tbs	3 Tbs
Medium onions, chopped	2	2
Garlic cloves, crushed	4	4
Fresh root ginger, peeled and finely chopped	2½cm/1in piece	1in piece
Green chillis, halved and seeded	6	6
Turmeric	1 tsp	1 tsp
Ground coriander	2 tsp	2 tsp
Black pepper	¼ tsp	¼ tsp
Thin coconut milk	300ml/10floz	1¼ cups
Cod steaks	1kg/2lb	2lb
Thick coconut milk	450ml/15floz	2 cups
Salt	1 tsp	1 tsp
Lemon juice	2 Tbs	2 Tbs
Sugar	1 tsp	1 tsp
Chopped coriander leaves	1 Tbs	1 Tbs

Heat the oil in a large saucepan. Add the onions and fry until they are golden brown. Add the garlic, ginger and chillis and fry for 3 minutes, stirring frequently. Add the turmeric, coriander and pepper and fry for 2 minutes. Pour over the thin coconut milk and stir to mix. Add the fish and bring to the boil. Cook for 5 minutes. Carefully stir in the thick coconut milk and salt and reduce the heat to low. Simmer for 20 minutes, or until the fish flakes easily. Remove from the heat and stir in the lemon juice and sugar.

Transfer the curry to a warmed serving dish. Sprinkle over the coriander leaves and serve at once.

6 Servings

JHINGA KARI I
(Prawn or Shrimp Curry)

This recipe is an adaptation of a recipe from the west coast of India, where large fresh prawns (shrimps) from the Indian Ocean are used. They are usually marinated in vinegar before being cooked; here we have suggested using cooked prawns or shrimps, more common in the West.

	Metric/U.K.	U.S.
Vegetable oil	50ml/2floz	4 Tbs
Fresh root ginger, peeled and finely chopped	4cm/1½in piece	1½in piece
Garlic cloves, crushed	3	3
Onions, finely chopped	3	3
Green chillis, finely chopped	3	3
Ground coriander	2 Tbs	2 Tbs
Turmeric	2 tsp	2 tsp
Wine vinegar	3 Tbs	3 Tbs
Salt	1 tsp	1 tsp
Large cooked prawns or shrimps, shelled	1kg/2lb	2lb
Hot coconut milk	450ml/15floz	2 cups

Heat the oil in a large saucepan. Add the ginger and garlic and fry for 1 minute, stirring constantly. Add the onions and fry until they are golden brown. Stir in the chillis and fry for 30 seconds. Stir in the coriander and turmeric, reduce the heat to moderately low and fry for a further 4 minutes, stirring constantly. Add the vinegar and salt and fry for 30 seconds.

Stir in the prawns or shrimps and fry for 2 to 3 minutes, stirring and tossing the prawns or shrimps until they are thoroughly coated. Pour in the milk, increase the heat to moderate and bring to the boil, stirring constantly. Reduce the heat to low, cover the pan and simmer the mixture for 5 minutes.

Transfer the curry to a warmed serving dish and serve at once.

6 Servings

Sondhia is a delicate dish of spiced large Dublin Bay prawns (large Gulf shrimps).

JHINGA KARI II
(Prawn or Shrimp and Vegetable Curry)

This colourful dish is both easy and quick to make —and is a meal in itself with plain boiled rice or lentils.

	Metric/U.K.	U.S.
Vegetable oil	3 Tbs	3 Tbs
Medium onions, chopped	2	2
Garlic cloves, crushed	2	2
Fresh root ginger, peeled and finely chopped	2½cm/1in piece	1in piece
Green chillis, seeded and finely chopped	2	2
Turmeric	1 tsp	1 tsp
Ground coriander	2 Tbs	2 Tbs
Paprika	2 tsp	2 tsp
Ground fennel	1 tsp	1 tsp
Aubergines (eggplants), cubed	2	2
Canned peeled tomatoes	425g/14oz	14oz
Salt	1 tsp	1 tsp
Creamed coconut	½cm/¼in slice	¼in slice
Juice of ½ lemon		
Water	300ml/10floz	1¼ cups
Prawns or shrimps, shelled	½kg/1lb	1lb
Green chillis, slit lengthways	2	2

Heat the oil in a large saucepan. Add the onions and fry until they are golden brown. Add the garlic, ginger and chopped chillis and fry for 3 minutes, stirring constantly. Stir in the turmeric, coriander, paprika and fennel and fry for 5 minutes, stirring frequently.

Add the aubergines (eggplants) and fry for 3 minutes, stirring frequently. Add the tomatoes and can juice, the salt, coconut, lemon juice and water, and bring to the boil, stirring constantly. Reduce the heat to low, cover the pan and simmer the curry for 30 minutes.

Stir in the prawns or shrimps and the two slit chillis. Re-cover and simmer for a further 15 minutes.

Transfer the curry to a warmed serving dish and serve at once.

4 Servings

SONDHIA
(Spiced Prawns or Shrimps)

Sondhia is a classic dish from the west coast of India.

	Metric/U.K.	U.S.
Uncooked Dublin Bay prawns (large Gulf shrimps)	1kg/2lb	2lb
Hot chilli powder	1 tsp	1 tsp
Ground cumin	1 tsp	1 tsp
Turmeric	2 tsp	2 tsp
Salt	1½ tsp	1½ tsp
Garlic cloves, crushed	3	3
Green chillis, finely chopped	3	3
Lemon juice	50ml/2floz	¼ cup
Water	300ml/10floz	1¼ cups
Vegetable oil	50ml/2floz	¼ cup
Finely chopped coriander leaves	2 Tbs	2 Tbs

Shell the prawns (shrimps) and reserve the shells. De-vein, then run the prawns (shrimps) under cold running water. Pat them dry with kitchen towels and transfer them to a large mixing bowl. Set aside.

Combine the chilli powder, cumin, turmeric, salt, garlic and chillis, then stir in just enough lemon juice to make a paste. Rub the paste into the prawns (shrimps) and set them aside for 1 hour.

Meanwhile, put the prawn (shrimp) shells and water into a saucepan and bring to the boil. Reduce the heat to low, cover the pan and simmer the shells for 20 minutes. Remove from the heat and strain the stock into a measuring cup. Discard the shells and reserve 250ml/8floz (1 cup) of strained stock.

Heat the oil in a large frying-pan. Add the prawns (shrimps), reduce the heat to low and simmer the prawns (shrimps), turning them occasionally, for 5 minutes, or until they turn pink. Stir in the reserved stock and bring to the boil. Reduce the heat to low and simmer for 20 minutes, stirring occasionally, or until the prawns (shrimps) are cooked through and tender. Stir in the remaining lemon juice and the coriander leaves.

Transfer the curry to a warmed serving dish and serve at once.

4-6 Servings

A colourful, satisfying mixture of vegetables, turmeric-flavoured rice and prawns (shrimps), that's Vegetable Pulao with Prawns or Shrimps.

JHINGA TIKKA
(Prawn or Shrimp Patties)

These little patties can either be served as part of an Indian meal, or as a snack or appetizer with drinks.

	Metric/U.K.	U.S.
Prawns or shrimps, shelled and chopped	275g/10oz	10oz
Medium onion, finely chopped	1	1
Fresh root ginger, peeled and finely chopped	1cm/½in piece	½in piece
Green chilli, chopped	1	1
Finely chopped coriander leaves	1 Tbs	1 Tbs
Salt	¾ tsp	¾ tsp
Lemon juice	1 Tbs	1 Tbs
Fresh white breadcrumbs	2 Tbs	2 Tbs
Turmeric	¼ tsp	¼ tsp
Black pepper	¼ tsp	¼ tsp
Egg	1	1

	Metric/U.K.	U.S.
Dry breadcrumbs	75g/3oz	1 cup
Vegetable oil	50ml/2floz	¼ cup

Put the prawns or shrimps, onion, ginger, chilli, coriander leaves, salt, lemon juice, fresh breadcrumbs, turmeric, pepper and egg into a mixing bowl and knead until the ingredients are well mixed. Divide the mixture into eight portions, then shape into flat, round patties.

Dip the patties in the dry breadcrumbs, coating them thoroughly and shaking off any excess.

Heat the oil in a large frying-pan. Add the patties and fry for 5 to 7 minutes on each side, or until they are golden brown and cooked through.

Transfer the patties to a warmed serving dish and serve at once.

4-6 Servings

VEGETABLE PULAU WITH PRAWNS OR SHRIMPS

	Metric/U.K.	U.S.
Large uncooked prawns or shrimps, shelled and de-veined	½kg/1lb	1lb
Salt	1½ tsp	1½ tsp
Cayenne pepper	½ tsp	½ tsp
Juice of ½ lemon		
Butter	40g/1½oz	3 Tbs
Medium onions, sliced	2	2
Garlic cloves, sliced	2	2
Cumin seeds	1 tsp	1 tsp
Turmeric	1 tsp	1 tsp
French beans, trimmed and sliced	125g/4oz	⅔ cup
Carrots, sliced	3	3
Small courgettes (zucchini), sliced	2	2
Long-grain rice, soaked in cold water for 30 minutes and drained	350g/12oz	2 cups
SAUCE		
Vegetable oil	2 Tbs	2 Tbs
Medium onion, chopped	1	1
Garlic clove, crushed	1	1
Fresh root ginger, peeled and finely chopped	4cm/1½in piece	1½in piece
Green chillis, chopped	2	2
Turmeric	1 tsp	1 tsp
Ground coriander	1 Tbs	1 Tbs
Cayenne pepper	½ tsp	½ tsp
Paprika	2 tsp	2 tsp
Canned peeled tomatoes, rubbed through a strainer with the can juice	700g/1½lb	1½ lb
Sugar	1 tsp	1 tsp
Salt	1 tsp	1 tsp
Creamed coconut	4cm/1½in slice	1½in slice

Put the prawns or shrimps on a plate and rub them all over with ½ teaspoon of salt, the cayenne and lemon juice. Set aside for 30 minutes.

Meanwhile, make the sauce. Heat the oil in a saucepan. Add the onion, garlic, ginger and chillis and fry until the onion is golden brown. Stir in the turmeric, coriander, cayenne and paprika. Cook for 2 minutes and add the strained tomatoes, sugar and salt. Bring to the boil. Reduce the heat to low, cover the pan and simmer the sauce for 20 minutes. Stir in the creamed coconut until it has dissolved, then bring to the boil again. Cover the pan and simmer for a further 20 minutes.

Meanwhile, melt the butter in a large saucepan. Add the prawns or shrimps and fry, turning them frequently, for 5 minutes, or until they turn slightly pink. Transfer to a plate. Add the onions and garlic to the pan and fry until the onions are golden brown. Add the cumin seeds and turmeric and stir to mix. Add the beans, carrots and courgettes (zucchini). Reduce the heat to low, cover the pan and simmer for 10 minutes, or until the vegetables are almost tender. Stir in the rice and remaining salt and fry for 2 minutes, stirring constantly. Return the prawns or shrimps to the pan and stir well. Pour over enough boiling water to cover the prawns or shrimps by about 1cm/½in. Bring to the boil, reduce the heat to low and cover the pan. Simmer for 15 to 20 minutes, or until the rice is tender and the liquid has been absorbed.

Transfer the rice mixture to a warmed serving dish. Pour the sauce into a warmed bowl and serve, with the rice mixture.

6 Servings

Accompaniments

ADRAK CHATNI
(Ginger Chutney)

This recipe is quick and easy to make, especially if you have a blender. It does not, however, keep very well and should be eaten within two days of preparation. It goes particularly well with lamb dishes.

	Metric/U.K.	U.S.
Juice of 2 lemons		
Sugar	4 tsp	4 tsp
Fresh root ginger, peeled and finely chopped	125g/4oz	4oz
Sultanas or seedless raisins	75g/3oz	½ cup
Garlic clove	1	1
Salt	1½ tsp	1½ tsp

Put the juice of 1½ lemons, 2 teaspoons of the sugar and all the remaining ingredients into a blender and blend to a smooth purée. Taste and, if necessary, stir in the juice of the remaining ½ lemon and the remaining sugar. Alternatively, chop all the ingredients finely and mix together.

Transfer the mixture to a small bowl and serve.

6 Servings

LIME PICKLE

	Metric/U.K.	U.S.
Whole limes	20	20
Green chillis	20	20
Coarse rock salt	6 Tbs	6 Tbs
Bay leaves, crumbled	4	4
Fresh root ginger, peeled and cut into thin matchstick shapes	175g/6oz	6oz
Lime juice	300ml/10floz	1¼ cups

Wash the limes in cold water and dry on kitchen towels. Make four cuts through the limes to quarter them to within ½cm/¼in of the bottom. Remove the pips (stones).

Slit the chillis lengthways and scrape out the seeds, leaving the chillis whole with their stalks.

Arrange a layer of limes on the bottom of a large pickling jar. Sprinkle with salt and crumbled bay leaves. Add 2 or 3 chillis and about 2 tablespoons of the ginger. Repeat these layers until all the ingredients, except half the salt, are used up. Pour over the lime juice and give the jar a good shake to settle the contents.

Cover the mouth of the jar with a clean cloth and tie in place with string. Put the jar in a sunny place for at least 6 days, adding half a tablespoon of the remaining salt each day. Shake the jar at least twice a day. Each night, put the jar in a dry place in the kitchen. Be sure to turn the jar each day so that all sides are exposed to the sun's rays.

After six days, keep the pickle on a shelf for 10 days. Cover with a lid and shake the jar every day. The pickle will be ready to eat after 10 days.

About 1½kg/3 pounds

TAMATAR CHATNI
(Tomato Chutney)

	Metric/U.K.	U.S.
Tomatoes, blanched, peeled and chopped	1kg/2lb	2lb
White wine vinegar	450ml/15floz	2 cups
Onions, finely chopped	2	2
Salt	1 Tbs	1 Tbs
Soft brown sugar	350g/12oz	2 cups
Fresh root ginger, peeled and finely chopped	5cm/2in piece	2in piece
Garlic cloves, finely chopped	4	4
Dried red chillis, finely chopped (or use 2 tsp hot chilli powder)	4	4
Whole cloves	12	12

A selection of the many spices used in Indian pickles and chutneys. It includes coconut, cumin seeds, coriander leaves, chillis, cloves, root ginger and garlic. The yellow powder to the left of the picture is turmeric.

	Metric/U.K.	U.S.
Cinnamon bark	2 pieces	2 pieces
Cardamom seeds, crushed	$\frac{1}{2}$ tsp	$\frac{1}{2}$ tsp
Vegetable oil	50ml/2floz	$\frac{1}{4}$ cup
Mustard seeds	1 Tbs	1 Tbs

No really good Indian meal is quite complete without the accompaniments, especially chutney. The particular chutney pictured here is Date and Banana.

Combine all the ingredients together, except the oil and mustard seeds, in a saucepan. Bring to the boil, reduce the heat to moderately low and simmer for 5 hours, stirring occasionally, or until the mixture is thick.

Meanwhile, heat the oil in a small frying-pan. Add the mustard seeds and cover. Fry until they begin to pop, then tip the seeds and oil into the saucepan. Cook for a further 15 minutes.

Remove from the heat and spoon the chutney into clean, dry jam or preserving jars. Serve when cool, or store, covered with vinegar-resistant paper, in a cool place or in the refrigerator.

About 400ml/14floz (1$\frac{3}{4}$ cups)

CUCUMBER CHUTNEY

	Metric/U.K.	U.S.
Small cucumber, peeled, finely chopped and dégorged	1	1
Large onion, finely chopped	1	1
Garlic clove, crushed	1	1
Salt and pepper to taste		
Wine vinegar	4 Tbs	4 Tbs

Combine all the ingredients together and beat well to blend.

Transfer the mixture to a small bowl and use as required.

6-8 Servings

DATE AND BANANA CHUTNEY

	Metric/U.K.	U.S.
Bananas, peeled and sliced	6	6
Medium onions, chopped	4	4
Dates, stoned (pitted) and chopped	225g/8oz	1$\frac{1}{3}$ cups
Vinegar	300ml/10floz	1$\frac{1}{4}$ cups
Ground coriander	$\frac{1}{2}$ tsp	$\frac{1}{2}$ tsp
Turmeric	$\frac{1}{4}$ tsp	$\frac{1}{4}$ tsp
Ground cumin	$\frac{1}{4}$ tsp	$\frac{1}{4}$ tsp
Ground ginger	$\frac{1}{4}$ tsp	$\frac{1}{4}$ tsp
Crystallized (candied) ginger, chopped	125g/4oz	4oz

	Metric/U.K.	U.S.
Salt	$\frac{1}{2}$ tsp	$\frac{1}{2}$ tsp
Black treacle or molasses	250ml/8floz	1 cup

Put the bananas, onions, dates and vinegar into a saucepan and cook for 15 minutes, stirring occasionally, or until the onions are cooked. Remove from the heat and mash to a pulp. Alternatively, put the mixture into a blender and blend to a purée.

Stir in the coriander, turmeric, cumin, ground ginger, crystallized (candied) ginger, salt and treacle or molasses and return the mixture to moderate heat. Cook for 15 to 20 minutes, stirring occasionally with a wooden spoon, or until the mixture is a rich brown colour.

Remove from the heat and spoon the chutney into clean, warmed jam or preserving jars. Cover with vinegar-resistant paper, cover, label and store in a cool, dry place until you wish to use.

About 1½kg/3 pounds

MANGO CHUTNEY

The cooking time for this chutney varies considerably depending on the quality of fruit used, and the yield given is therefore only approximate for the same reason. This chutney improves with keeping and should be stored for three or four weeks before using.

	Metric/U.K.	U.S.
Green mangoes, peeled, halved and stoned (pitted)	1½kg/3lb	3lb
Salt	6 Tbs	6 Tbs
Water	1¾l/3 pints	4 pints
Sugar	½kg/1lb	2 cups
Vinegar	600ml/1 pint	2½ cups
Fresh root ginger, peeled and finely chopped	75g/3oz	3oz
Garlic cloves, finely chopped	10	10
Hot chilli powder	2 tsp	2 tsp
Cinnamon stick	1x10cm/4in	1x4in
Raisins	125g/4oz	$\frac{2}{3}$ cup
Stoned (pitted) dates, chopped	125g/4oz	$\frac{2}{3}$ cup

Cut the mangoes into cubes. Dissolve the salt in the water in a large bowl. Stir in the mango cubes, cover and set aside at room temperature for 24 hours. Drain the cubes in a colander and set aside.

Dissolve the sugar in the vinegar over low heat, stirring frequently. When it has dissolved, bring the mixture to the boil. Add the mango cubes, ginger, garlic, chilli powder, cinnamon, raisins and dates and bring back to the boil, stirring occasionally. Reduce the heat to moderately low and simmer the chutney for 1½ to 2 hours, or until it is thick.

Remove from the heat. Remove the cinnamon stick. Spoon the chutney into clean, warmed jam or preserving jars. Cover with vinegar-resistant paper, cover, label and store in a cool, dry place until you wish to use.

About 2kg/4 pounds

TAMARIND SAUCE

This sweet-sour sauce from southern India is often served with Pakoras (page 6). If raw sugar is unobtainable, use soft brown sugar or molasses or dark treacle instead.

	Metric/U.K.	U.S.
Tamarind	225g/8oz	1 cup
Boiling water	900ml/1½ pints	3¾ cups
Salt	1 tsp	1 tsp
Fresh root ginger, peeled and finely chopped	2½cm/1in piece	1in piece
Raw sugar	2 Tbs	2 Tbs
Hot chilli powder	1 tsp	1 tsp

Put the tamarind into a bowl and pour over the boiling water. Set aside until the mixture is cool. Pour the mixture through a fine strainer into a saucepan, using the back of a wooden spoon to push through as much of the softened tamarind pulp as possible. Discard the contents of the strainer. Stir the salt, ginger, sugar and chilli powder into the pan and simmer gently for 20 minutes, stirring occasionally.

Remove from the heat and spoon into a warmed sauceboat. Set aside to cool slightly before serving.

About 425ml/14floz (1¾ cups)

RAITA I
(Yogurt Salad)

	Metric/U.K.	U.S.
Yogurt	600ml/1 pint	2½ cups
Cucumber, washed, sliced and dégorged	½	½
Spring onions, (scallions), finely chopped	4	4
Salt and pepper to taste		
Green chilli, finely chopped	1	1
Paprika	¼ tsp	¼ tsp

Put the yogurt into a mixing bowl and beat

until it is smooth. Stir in the cucumber, spring onions (scallions), and seasoning to taste. Pour the mixture into a serving bowl.

Cover the bowl and chill in the refrigerator for 1 hour, or until thoroughly chilled. Remove from the refrigerator and discard the covering. Sprinkle over the chilli and paprika and serve.

4-6 Servings

RAITA II
(Yogurt Salad)

If fresh mangoes are unavailable, this raita tastes just as good with canned ones. Or substitute guavas if you prefer.

	Metric/U.K.	U.S.
Yogurt	600ml/1 pint	$2\frac{1}{2}$ cups
Ripe fresh mangoes, peeled, stoned and diced	2	2
Salt	$\frac{1}{2}$ tsp	$\frac{1}{2}$ tsp
Ghee or clarified butter	1 Tbs	1 Tbs
Mustard seeds	1 tsp	1 tsp
Green chilli, finely chopped	1	1
Finely chopped coriander leaves	2 tsp	2 tsp

Put the yogurt into a mixing bowl and beat until it is smooth. Stir in the mangoes and salt. Set aside.

Melt the ghee or clarified butter in a small frying-pan. Add the mustard seeds and cover. Fry until they begin to pop. Add the chilli and fry for 20 seconds, stirring constantly. Remove from the heat and stir the mustard and chilli mixture into the yogurt. Stir well to mix. Pour the mixture into a serving bowl.

Cover the bowl and chill in the refrigerator for 1 hour, or until thoroughly chilled. Remove from the refrigerator and discard the covering. Sprinkle over the coriander leaves and serve at once.

4-6 Servings

SAMBAL I

This sambal is usually served with fish or vegetable curries.

	Metric/U.K.	U.S.
Peeled cooked shrimps, chopped	175g/6oz	6oz
Hard-boiled eggs, sliced	2	2
Medium onion, finely chopped	1	1
Green chilli, finely chopped	1	1
Fresh root ginger, peeled	$2\frac{1}{2}$cm/1in	1in

Indian 'salads' are usually yogurt based and provide a cool, refreshing complement to the hotter, spicier dishes. Two particularly delightful raitas are pictured here: on the left Raita I, with yogurt, cucumber and spring onions (scallions) and Raita II, yogurt, mangoes and mustard seeds.

	Metric/U.K.	U.S.
and finely chopped	piece	piece
Hot chilli powder	$\frac{1}{4}$ tsp	$\frac{1}{4}$ tsp
Thick coconut milk	2 Tbs	2 Tbs
Cumin seeds, coarsely crushed	$\frac{1}{4}$ tsp	$\frac{1}{4}$ tsp

Combine all the ingredients, except the cumin seeds, in a shallow serving dish and mix well. Sprinkle the crushed cumin seeds over the top.

Cover the bowl and chill in the refrigerator until you are ready to serve.

3-4 Servings

Sambals also make popular accompaniments to various Indian dishes— on the left, a pungent mixture of shrimps, hard-boiled eggs and onion, and on the right a mixture of tomatoes, onion and grated or desiccated (shredded) coconut.

SAMBAL II

	Metric/U.K.	U.S.
Medium tomatoes, blanched, peeled and chopped	2	2
Medium onion, finely chopped	1	1
Green chilli, finely chopped	1	1
Lime or lemon juice	2 Tbs	2 Tbs
Salt and pepper to taste		
Grated fresh coconut or desiccated (shredded) coconut	2 Tbs	2 Tbs

Combine the tomatoes, onion and chilli in a small bowl. Pour over the lime or lemon juice and season to taste. Spoon into a shallow serving dish and scatter over the coconut.

Cover the bowl and chill in the refrigerator until you are ready to serve.

3-4 Servings

Breads

PURIS
(Deep-fried Bread)

	Metric/U.K.	U.S.
Wholewheat (wholemeal) flour	225g/8oz	2 cups
Salt	½ tsp	½ tsp
Ghee or clarified butter	1 Tbs	1 Tbs
Warm water	50ml/2floz	¼ cup
Sufficient vegetable oil for deep-frying		

Combine the flour and salt in a bowl. Add the ghee or clarified butter and, using your fingertips, rub into the flour until it is absorbed. Add the water and, using your hands, knead the mixture until it forms a stiff dough, adding more water if necessary.

Turn the dough out on to a lightly floured board and knead it for 10 minutes, or until it is smooth and elastic.

Shape into a ball, return to the bowl, cover and set aside at room temperature for 30 minutes.

Turn out on to the floured board and pinch off small pieces of the dough. Roll them into balls, then flatten and roll out into rounds about 10cm/4in in diameter.

Fill a deep-frying pan one-third full with oil and heat until it reaches 180°C (350°F) on a deep-fat thermometer, or until a small piece of stale bread dropped into the oil turns golden in 55 seconds.

Carefully lower the rounds, one or two at a time, into the oil and, using a fish slice or spatula, press down. Fry for 1 minute, turn over and press down again. Fry for 30 seconds or until the puri is puffed up and golden brown.

Remove from the pan and drain on kitchen towels. Serve hot or warm.

About 12 Puris

One of the more exotic Indian breads, deep-fried Puris, made from wholewheat (wholemeal) flour.

Two of the most popular Indian breads—Paratha and Chappatis.

PARATHAS
(Fried Wholewheat Bread)

Paratha is a layered fried bread, formed by brushing the dough with ghee or clarified butter and folding and rolling it a number of times. The dough may be prepared in advance and kept for several hours in the refrigerator, covered with a damp cloth. They can also be cooked, then re-heated either in the frying-pan or in a hot oven before serving.

	Metric/U.K.	U.S.
Wholewheat (wholemeal) flour	225g/8oz	2 cups
Salt	1 tsp	1 tsp
Ghee or clarified butter	125g/4oz	8 Tbs
Water	50-125ml/ 2-4floz	$\frac{1}{4}$-$\frac{1}{2}$ cup

Combine the flour and salt in a bowl. Add 2 tablespoons of the ghee or clarified butter and, using your fingertips, rub the butter into the flour until it is absorbed. Pour in 50ml/2floz ($\frac{1}{4}$ cup) of the water and, using your hands, knead the mixture until it forms a soft dough. If it is too dry, add the remaining water, a little at a time, until the dough is soft and comes away from the sides of the bowl.

Turn out on to a lightly floured board and knead for 10 minutes, or until it is smooth and elastic. Pat into a ball and return to the bowl. Cover and set aside at room temperature for 1 hour.

Turn the dough out on to the floured board and divide into four portions. Shape each portion into a ball and roll out into a thin round shape. Brush each round with a little of the remaining ghee or clarified butter. Fold the rounds in half, then in quarters. Roll out into rounds again, brush with a little more of the ghee or butter, fold and repeat the process again until all but 2 tablespoons of the ghee or clarified butter has been used up.

Now roll out each dough piece into a round about 18cm/7in in diameter.

Using a little of the remaining ghee or clarified butter, lightly grease a heavy frying-pan and heat it over moderate heat. Add a paratha and cook it, moving it with your fingertips occasionally, for 3 to 4 minutes, or until the underside is lightly browned. Brush the top of the paratha with a little of the remaining clarified butter, turn over and continue cooking for a further 2 to 3 minutes or until it is browned all over.

Remove from the pan and keep hot while you cook the remaining parathas in the same way.

Serve hot.

4 Parathas

CHAPPATIS
(Unleavened Bread)

Chappatis is probably the most popular of all the Indian breads and, although you can obtain them ready-made from Indian provision stores or even the larger supermarkets, it is very easy to make your own—and much more satisfying, of course! Serve them instead of rice for a lighter meal, or with a selection of dishes.

	Metric/U.K.	U.S.
Wholewheat (wholemeal) flour	225g/8oz	2 cups
Salt	$\frac{1}{2}$ tsp	$\frac{1}{2}$ tsp
Butter or vegetable fat	50g/2oz	4 Tbs
Water	150ml/5floz	$\frac{5}{8}$ cup
Ghee or clarified butter, melted	1 Tbs	1 Tbs

Pour the flour and salt into a bowl. Add the butter or fat and rub into the flour with your fingertips. Make a well in the centre and pour in 75ml/3floz ($\frac{3}{8}$ cup) of the water. Mix with your fingers and add the rest of the water gradually. Form the dough into a ball and turn out on to a lightly floured board. Knead the dough for 10 minutes, or until it becomes smooth and elastic. Put the dough into a bowl, cover and set aside at room temperature for 30 minutes.

Turn out on to a floured board and divide the dough into eight portions. Roll out each piece into a thin, round shape, about the size of a small plate.

Meanwhile, heat a heavy frying-pan over moderate heat. Put one portion of dough in the pan and, when small blisters appear on the surface, press the chappati to flatten it. Turn over and cook until it is a pale golden colour.

Remove the chappati from the pan and brush with a little ghee or clarified butter. Put on a plate and cover with a second plate to keep hot until all the chappatis are cooked. Serve warm.

8 Chappatis

Sweetmeats

GULAB JAMUN
(Deep-fried Dough Balls)

Desserts in the western sense are unknown in India but there is a natural sweet tooth—as can be seen from the selection of sweetmeats which follows. Sweetmeats are traditionally served after the main meal in India.

	Metric/U.K.	U.S.
Powdered milk	125g/4oz	½ cup
Flour	2 Tbs	2 Tbs
Baking powder	1 tsp	1 tsp
Ghee or clarified butter, melted	1 Tbs	1 Tbs
Water	50ml/2floz	¼ cup
Sufficient vegetable oil for deep-frying		
SYRUP Sugar	225g/8oz	1 cup
Boiling water	125ml/4floz	½ cup

First make the syrup. Dissolve the sugar in the water over moderate heat, stirring constantly. Simmer for 10 minutes, stirring frequently with a wooden spoon, or until the mixture has thickened slightly.

Meanwhile, combine all the dry ingredients together, and, using your fingertips, beat in the ghee or clarified butter. Add the water and knead until the mixture forms a slightly soft dough. Set aside at room temperature for 30 minutes. Using your hands, shape the mixture into small balls.

Fill a deep-frying pan one-third full with oil and heat until it reaches 180°C (350°F) on a deep-fat thermometer, or until a small cube of stale bread dropped into the oil turns golden in 55 seconds. Carefully lower the balls into the oil, a few at a time, and fry for 3 to 4 minutes, or until they are golden brown and crisp, and rise to the surface. As they brown, transfer the balls to the syrup mixture. When all the balls are cooked, remove the syrup from the heat and set aside to cool.

Chill in the refrigerator for at least 30 minutes before serving.

4-6 Servings

HALVA
(Semolina Dessert)

	Metric/U.K.	U.S.
Sugar	400g/14oz	1¾ cups
Cardamom seeds	4	4
Cinnamon sticks	3x10cm/4in	3x4in
Butter	225g/8oz	16 Tbs
Semolina	225g/8oz	2 cups
Sultanas or seedless raisins	125g/4oz	⅔ cup
Blanched almonds, slivered	125g/4oz	1 cup

Dissolve the sugar in 900ml/1½ pints (3¾ cups) of boiling water and add the cardamom and cinnamon. Cook for 10 minutes, or until the mixture becomes syrupy.

Melt the butter in a second saucepan and stir in the semolina. Simmer for 20 minutes, stirring frequently. Add the sultanas or seedless raisins, almonds and the sugar syrup and bring to the boil. Boil for 5 minutes, stirring constantly. Discard the cardamom and cinnamon.

Pour the mixture into a shallow dish and set aside to cool.

Serve cold.

4-6 Servings

KULFI
(Ice-Cream)

	Metric/U.K.	U.S.
Mango juice	450ml/15floz	2 cups
Double (heavy) cream	150ml/5floz	⅝ cup
Sugar	2 Tbs	2 Tbs

Combine all the ingredients and spoon the mixture into six small moulds. Tightly cover with foil and put into the freezing compartment of the refrigerator. Shake the moulds three times during the first hour of freezing.

When the mixture is firm and set, remove from the refrigerator and dip the bottoms quickly in boiling water. Invert on to serving plates, giving the moulds a sharp shake. Serve at once.

6 Servings

A selection of popular Indian sweetmeats—top left Halva, a semolina fudge like dessert; centre Gulab Jamun, small deep-fried dough balls in syrup; and bottom left Kulfi, mango juice ice-cream.

Glossary

Asafoetida: Dried gum resin used as a spice in Indian cooking. Obtainable from Indian provision stores. No substitute, but it may be omitted from any recipe if it is unobtainable.

Chick-Pea Flour: Used extensively for batters in Indian cooking. Sold as *gram* or *besan* flour from Indian provision stores. Or you can grind chick-peas, then sift, until they are sufficiently refined.

Chilli: Small hot red or green pepper, often used in Indian cooking. Obtainable from Indian or Mexican provision stores. To reduce the fieriness of any dish, either reduce the number of chillis used, or seed them before adding them to the dish (the seeds are the hottest part). If fresh or dried chillis are not available, hot chilli powder may be substituted: allow about ½ teaspoon per 1 chilli. When preparing chillis for cooking, always wear rubber gloves for protection and chop, seed etc well away from your eyes.

Coconut Milk: The milk of the coconut. If unobtainable, an acceptable substitute can be made by dissolving creamed coconut in boiling water. Use about 5cm/2in slice for every 450ml/15floz (2 cups) of water and stir until it dissolves. For thick coconut milk, add a little extra creamed coconut, for thin milk, a little less.

Coriander Leaves: Used as a condiment in Indian cooking. A member of the parsley family, and chopped parsley makes an acceptable substitute, especially if it is to be sprinkled over food after it has been cooked. Fresh coriander leaves can be obtained from Indian, Greek or Mexican food stores.

Curry Powder: Virtually unknown in India, but can be used as a short-cut to cooking Indian dishes. Available, in various strengths, from delicatessens or supermarkets. What is sold as curry powder is usually a combination of coriander, cumin, turmeric and hot chilli powder, perhaps with ground ginger and other spices as well.

Dhal: The word used to describe legumes or pulses. Lentils, which are a type of dhal, come in many varieties in India and form an important part of the diet, especially in the South. Substitute with any type of lentil obtainable in the West if you cannot find the Indian types mentioned.

Garam Masala: A type of 'dry' masala or mixture of ground spices. Sold commercially in Indian provision stores and larger supermarkets. To make your own, experiment with combinations of black pepper, cumin, cinnamon, cardamom, cloves, nutmeg and coriander.

Ghee: A type of clarified butter very popular in Indian cooking. Available in cans from Indian provision stores. To make at home, put about 450g/1lb (2 cups) of butter into a heavy-based saucepan and melt very slowly over low heat, being careful not to let it brown. Heat to just below boiling point then simmer for 30 minutes, or until the moisture in the butter evaporates and the protein sinks to the bottom, leaving the pure clear fat on top. Remove the pan from the heat and carefully strain the clear fat through several thicknesses of cheesecloth into a jar. Cover tightly and store in a cool place. It will solidify as it cools.

Ginger root: Knobbly and light brown, root ginger is an almost indispensable ingredient in Indian cooking. It can be readily obtained from Indian provision stores, or oriental delicatessens (it is widely used in Chinese cooking, too). To store fresh ginger, wrap it tightly, unpeeled, in plastic film and store in the refrigerator for up to six weeks. If fresh ginger is unobtainable, ground ginger can be substituted, although the taste is not quite the same: use about ½ teaspoonful to 4cm/1½in piece of root ginger.

Pannir: A white curd cheese used for cooking in India. It is made from milk, soured milk and lemon juice. *Feta*, a Greek cheese, is somewhat similar in texture and can be substituted, as can any type of goat's cheese.

Tamarind: The dried fruit of the tamarind tree, which is used in South Indian cooking. The pulp is soaked in hot water and the seeds and fibre extracted before being used.

Yogurt: natural (plain) yogurt is a very popular ingredient in many Indian dishes and although commercial yogurt can be used, it is quite easy to make your own. Pour 1¼l/2 pints (5 cups) of milk into a saucepan and bring to the boil. Remove from the heat and cool to 43°C (110°F) on a sugar thermometer, or until you can immerse a finger in the liquid for 10 seconds without discomfort. Meanwhile, beat 2 tbs of yogurt or yogurt culture until it is smooth, then beat in 3 tbs of the warmed milk until blended, then cover, wrap in a towel and keep in a warm, draught-free place for 8 hours, or until thickened. Store in the refrigerator until ready to use.